Basic
FLY TYING

Basic
FLY TYING

All the Skills and Tools You Need to Get Started

Jon Rounds, editor

Wayne Luallen,
fly tier and consultant

Photographs by
Michael Radencich

Illustrations by John McKim

STACKPOLE
BOOKS

Copyright © 2002 by Stackpole Books

Published by
STACKPOLE BOOKS
5067 Ritter Road
Mechanicsburg, PA 17055
www.stackpolebooks.com

Printed in China

10 9 8 7 6 5 4 3 2

First edition

Photographs by Michael Radencich
Illustrations by John McKim
Illustrations on page 7 reprinted from *Fly Tying: Adventures
in Fur, Feathers and Fun* by John McKim, by permission of
Mountain Press Publishing Company

Library of Congress Cataloging-in-Publication Data

Basic fly tying / Jon Rounds, editor.— 1st ed.
      p. cm.
   Includes bibliographical references (p.).
   ISBN 0-8117-2473-5 (pbk.)
   1. Fly tying. I. Rounds, Jon.

SH451 .B27 2002
688.7'9124—dc21

                                                        2002021228

Contents

Acknowledgments

This book is based on the work of three extraordinary contributors. Wayne Luallen tied the flies on these pages, and it is his vast experience and skill on which the instruction is based. Michael Radencich shot the photographs and proved once again why he's the best in the business. John McKim created the illustrations, which articulate fine points of the tying process that photos alone could not. Michael and John, it must be noted, are also expert fly tiers and authors of books on tying. Along with Wayne, they formed a core of expertise that informs every page of this book. Any errors are mine.

Thanks for advice and instruction to:

Marvin Nolte; Herb and Cathy Weigl of Cold Spring Anglers; Bill and Emily Zeiders, Dusty Weidner, and Mark Altland of Yellow Breeches Outfitters; Jay Nichols of *Fly Fisherman* magazine.

Thanks also to Bill Chase of Anglers Sport Group, for providing Daiichi hooks; Christopher Helm of Whitetail Fly Tieing Supplies, Terry Ball of Nature's Spirit, and Lynelle Norton, for providing tying materials; Dr. Tom Whiting of Whiting Farms, for lending his exquisite genetic hackle; and Ron Abby of Abby Precision Manufacturing, for the loan of Dyna King vises.

—Jon Rounds

Introduction

This book is for beginners—those who have never tied a fly or who have begun tying but still want a clear, detailed, step-by-step guide. We further assume that the person who buys this book wants to tie flies to fish with them and have thus built it around sequential instructions for seven effective and popular patterns.

Several criteria influenced the selection of the patterns. First, they had to be relatively simple to tie. Second, they had to be proven on the water, patterns that expert fly fishers actually carry in their own boxes. We included no patterns simply because they're standard fare in beginner's books or because they illustrate a particular technique that old-school tiers insist is required knowledge. Finally, we wanted a range of pattern styles—nymphs, dries, and streamers—not only to teach the various skills required for these styles, but also to equip the beginner with a useful, balanced fly box.

The craft of fly tying is rich and deep. You can tie for a lifetime and keep discovering techniques and refining skills. If you watch four experts dub a body or tie in a wing, you'll likely see four slightly different approaches. This book does not attempt to cover every technique you'll ever need or every approach to every problem. And we don't want to suggest that any recipe here is so rigid that you shouldn't experiment or improvise.

What we do propose is that with no previous experience you'll be able to tie the patterns in this book, and that having done so, you'll have not only some great flies, but a solid set of skills on which to build.

1
Tools and Materials

TOOLS

You can begin with a modest kit. Don't be intimidated by the vast number and high prices of fly-tying tools. Most of the tools you'll see in catalogs and fly shops aren't necessary for the basics and will result in no better flies than those tied with fewer and simpler tools. The seven tools shown in this chapter are all you need to tie the patterns in this book and many more. As you progress, you can upgrade your kit and add any number of gadgets.

If you have a limited budget, spend most of it on a good vise, quality scissors, and a good bobbin. You'll use these three tools constantly, and cheap models will affect the quality of your flies and the ease of your tying.

Beginner's kits, with vise and all the tools in this chapter, are available in catalogs and fly shops, starting at about $40. A better way is to assemble your own kit from tools at the fly shop. This takes a little more time, but it allows you to handle individual tools before buying and to ask for advice. Fly shop owners and sales-people tend to be knowledgeable and helpful.

VISE

The vise is the most costly tool. It's main job is to hold the hook securely in place while you tie. The cheapest vises may not perform even this basic job well enough, but there are beginner's models in the $50 range that do it perfectly. A cam-operated stationary vise with a C-clamp base will serve you well.

Jaw Systems

The jaws are the two mated pieces of metal that hold the hook. Those on a very cheap vise may be of inferior metal and not machined accurately enough to hold the thin wire of a small hook securely.

Cam-operated. The most common type. The jaws are closed by flipping a lever. Jaws must first be adjusted to the diameter of the hook, but once adjusted, you can mount other hooks of the same size very quickly, a handy feature when tying several flies of the same type.

Screw-tightened. Jaws are closed by tightening a knob. This system works fine but is not as quick as the lever system when changing hooks of the same size.

The Thompson Pro Vise, above (about $38) and the Dyna-King Squire, right (about $150) have cam-operated jaws and C-clamp bases.

Bases

Vises are equipped with either a clamp or a pedestal base.

C-Clamp. Attaches to the edge of a table. Makes a very stable base if properly tightened, and also has the advantage of light weight. Most beginners buy this type. It can be used as a travel vise if you later buy a pedestal vise for home use. It also can be easily adjusted for height. The disadvantages are the limitations on where you can set it up. It must be mounted at the edge of a table, and the tabletop cannot be too thin or too thick for the base clamp.

Pedestal. Sits on top of the table on a heavy metal base. The big advantage is convenience. You simply set it down where you want to tie. Not quite as secure as a tightly clamped base, but plenty stable enough for tying small and medium-size flies. One slight disadvantage is that the height is not adjustable.

Stationary or Rotary

The jaws of a stationary vise are fixed in one position. Those on a rotary vise rotate 360 degrees, so the fly can be spun on its axis, a feature that makes some tying procedures quicker and easier and also allows the fly to be viewed from all angles. Most serious tiers use rotary vises, but some veterans stick with stationary. Rotary vises are significantly more expensive, and they aren't necessary to learn the basics. However, if you can afford one, there are no disadvantages to a rotary design, and it can easily be used as a stationary vise.

Dyna-King Squire

SCISSORS

A pair of sharp, well-made scissors is essential for the delicate and precise work of cutting fly-tying materials. Choose a pair that fits your hand comfortably. They should have finger holes large enough to slide up over your knuckles so you can keep the scissors in your hand, out of the way, while tying and then slide them down into position when you need to trim something. Some tiers keep scissors in hand for the entire tying operation.

Make sure the tips mate exactly when closed, as you will use the very ends to snip thread and fine material.

Many tiers keep a second, heavier pair of scissors for cutting coarse hair, synthetic materials, and wire. A pair of toenail clippers can also be used for cutting tinsel and wire. If you start with one pair of scissors, make sure to cut heavy material at the base of the blades so as not to dull or misalign the tips.

BOBBIN

Along with the vise and scissors, the bobbin is the third tool constantly in use when tying. You use it to wrap thread around the hook and then let it hang as a weight to hold material in place. The bobbin's critical function is to release thread under the proper tension. This tension can be adjusted by spreading or closing the wire arms (see page 12). The best bobbins have ceramic tubes (or metal tubes lined with ceramic). This material won't become grooved over time and start breaking thread as you tie.

A bobbin threader is a handy tool that helps you pull the thread through the small tube when you load a new spool onto the bobbin. Several types are available from catalogs and shops, but a dental floss threader—a loop of stiff monofilament with a tag end—works fine. You can get a lifetime supply for a few dollars in a supermarket or pharmacy.

dental floss threader

WHIP FINISHER

The whip finish is a knot used to finish a fly and sometimes to secure material when you're midway through a pattern. It can be tied by hand, but a tool invented by Frank Matarelli simplifies the process. Whip finishers are now available from several manufacturers, but the Matarelli style is the easiest to use.

HACKLE PLIERS

This tool is used to grasp the tip of a feather and wrap it around the hook to form the hackle of a fly. The only real requirements are that the pliers fit your hand and have enough tension to hold a feather tip securely. Beware of cheap models with rough-edged jaws that can break a fine hackle feather. Also, avoid miniature pliers. They can be awkward to use and may not be heavy enough for those times when you let the pliers dangle from the hook to hold a wrapped hackle in place.

BODKIN

Basically a thick needle mounted in a handle, a bodkin is used for a number of jobs, from dabbing on head cement to teasing fibers from dubbing material. It need not be expensive.

HAIR STACKER

A small cylinder used to align the tips of a bundle of hair. Animal hairs occur in different lengths on the hide, but for making a wing or tail, you often need hair of uniform length. To use the tool, you cut a bunch of hair from the hide, insert it tips-down in the barrel of the stacker, place the cap on, and tap the tool on the bench. This action aligns the tips of individual hairs by forcing them to the bottom of the cylinder. You then take off the cap and remove the stacked hair.

DUBBING TWISTER

A dubbing twister is used to spin a length of dubbing material into a twisted strand before it is wrapped around the hook. You can dub without a tool, but the dubbing twister is useful with coarse or wiry fibers or when a fly body requires some bulk. There are a number of styles on the market. Don't spend more than a few dollars on your first one. They all work.

HOOKS

A hook's size and shape must be appropriate for the insect or baitfish the fly imitates. You can't tie a realistic nymph imitation on a streamer hook because the shank's too long, and you shouldn't tie a dry fly on a heavy nymph hook because the fly won't float. Furthermore, the proportions of the fly are keyed to the size of the hook. For example, Woolly Bugger instructions say to cut the tail to the length of the hook shank and to select a hackle feather with barbs about 1¹/₂ to 2 times as long as the width of the hook gap.

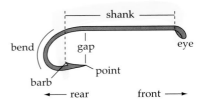

"Shank" is a general term for the straight portion of the hook, but in tying directions, "shank length" refers to the distance from the rear of the eye to a point directly above the barb.

The width of the gap is used as a reference against which to measure the length of hackle barbs for a particular fly.

In tying instructions, "forward" means toward the eye, and "rearward" means toward the bend.

Size

The larger the number, the smaller the hook. A size 28 hook is tiny and a size 1, relatively large. After size 1, the designations switch to 1/0, 2/0, and so on, and the system reverses: the larger the number, the larger the hook. Most trout flies range between size 16 and size 8, with 14 being the most common. Midges can be tied down to speck-sized 32, while giant saltwater streamers range up to size 4/0 and larger.

For each hook size there is a "standard" length as well as longer and shorter versions. Variations in length are expressed by a number and an X (like the multiplication symbol), signifying how much longer the hook is than standard. For example, a size 14 "1X long" dry fly hook is a little bit longer than a size 14 standard dry fly hook, a "2X long," longer still. Streamer hooks are typically "3X" or "4X long," because streamers imitate baitfish, whose bodies are longer than most insects'. Conversely, a "1X short" hook is a bit shorter than standard and is used for tying stubby nymphs and the like.

The same system applies to thickness of the hook wire. A "1X fine" hook is a little lighter gauge wire than standard, and a "1X heavy" ("strong" or "stout") a bit heavier. Dry fly hooks are "1X fine," because a dry fly must be very light, for buoyancy. Wet fly or nymph hooks are typically "1X" or "2X heavy," because these flies must sink.

Be aware that there is no universal set of standards used by all hook manufacturers, so you can expect slight variations in size between models from different makers.

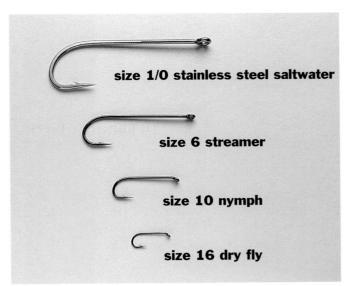

size 1/0 stainless steel saltwater

size 6 streamer

size 10 nymph

size 16 dry fly

THREAD

The most common sizes are 3/0, 6/0, and 8/0. The higher the number, the finer the thread. For most trout flies, 6/0 is a good choice. Size 14 and smaller flies may call for 8/0 thread because it produces a neater body with less thread buildup, but this finer thread is a little harder to work with at first and breaks more easily than 6/0. Size 3/0 thread is noticeably thicker and is used for streamers and bulky flies.

Most fly-tying thread is prewaxed for ease of handling.

Black, tan, and olive are the most common colors of thread. If you tie often, you'll find it handy to buy extra bobbins and load them with these colors so you don't have to rethread each time you need a different color.

marabou

turkey
tail
feather

pheasant
tail feather

FEATHERS

Sections of feathers are used for the bodies, wings, and tails of flies and are obtained from a wide variety of birds. The patterns in this book include feathers from chicken, turkey, pheasant and peacock. Examining feathers in detail is beyond the scope of this book, but knowing the basics of hackle—one of the most important and expensive types of feather in fly tying—is useful to the beginner.

HACKLE

The term "hackle" is used three ways. It's the generic name for the long, thin feathers from a domestic fowl's neck or its "saddle," the area on the back above the tail. It also refers to the part of a fly created when such a feather is wrapped around the body, causing the fibers to stick out at 90 degrees from the hook. Finally, it's used as a verb: to hackle a fly.

Hackle is sold as a neck or "cape," as a saddle, and as prepackaged individual feathers (the most expensive option). Each cape or saddle has enough feathers for many flies. Dry flies demand the highest quality hackle, fibers ("barbs") that are stiff, long, and consistent, and have supple stems. Domestic chickens have been selectively bred for decades to develop premium dry fly hackle, and the highest quality capes now cost more than $100 each. Rooster neck and saddle feathers are the best for dry fly hackle because their barbs are very stiff and thus keep the fly afloat.

Feathers from hen chicken necks and saddles are shorter and have more web—the soft barbules near the stem—and are better for wings and wet fly hackle than for dry fly hackle. Body feathers from grouse, partridge and other birds are also used for wet fly and nymph hackle, because they're softer than rooster hackle and tend to absorb water.

© *Fly Tying: Adventures in Fur, Feathers and Fun* by John Mckim Missoula, Montana: Mountain Press Publishing Co.

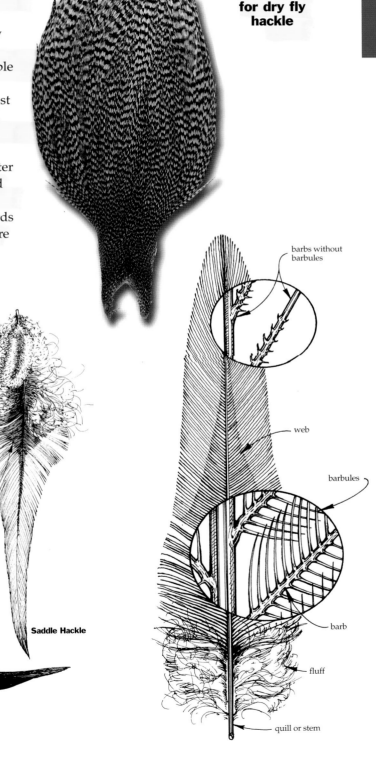

rooster neck (or "cape") for dry fly hackle

Spade Hackle

web

fluff

fluff

Saddle Hackle

web

web

Neck Hackle

web

fluff

fluff

Spey Hackle

all web

Hackle feathers from a rooster or gamecock

barbs without barbules

web

barbules

barb

fluff

quill or stem

Anatomy of a hackle feather

hare's mask

deer hair

elk hair

HAIR AND FUR

Natural hair and fur, such as that from rabbit, muskrat, beaver, deer, and elk, is used to make bodies, wings, and tails. As it occurs on the hide, mammal hair is a mixture of short, soft underfur, and long, stiff guard hairs. Underfur and guard hairs are sometimes mixed together to make fly bodies, but in other cases, one or the other is used alone. The fur from rabbit, muskrat and beaver is used to make bodies (see dubbing, below), while the hair from deer and elk is commonly used for wings and tails.

DUBBING

Dubbing is material that's wrapped around the hook shank to imitate the body of an aquatic insect. Dubbing can be made from natural fur and hair, synthetic material, or a blend of the two. It is twisted onto the tying thread and then wrapped around the hook.

Most tiers—and especially beginners—find natural material, such as rabbit or muskrat fur, easier to work with than synthetics, because it adheres to thread more readily. Natural material also contains a subtle mix of colors which tend to imitate an insect body more accurately than material dyed a uniform shade.

If you don't want to mix your own, pre-packaged natural, synthetic, and natural-synthetic dubbing blends are widely available in an array of colors. Synthetics, such as Antron yarn, add a touch of sparkle to the mix.

For many tiers, part of the fascination of fly tying is trying to match insects they find on the stream. They experiment with dubbing materials, mixing them in various shades and textures until they find what works.

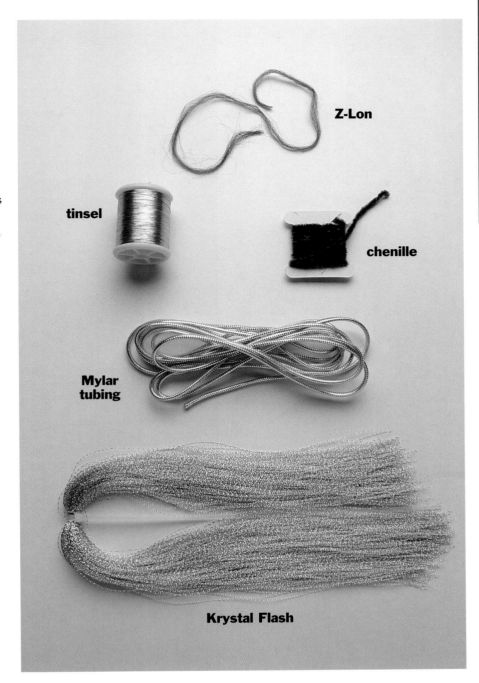

SYNTHETIC MATERIALS

A growing array of synthetic materials have been created or adapted for use in fly tying. Some synthetics are not as easy to handle as natural materials or do not perform as well in the water. Others have become standard, in some cases to replace natural material from species that are now protected, and in other cases simply because they work better than anything else. Among the synthetics used in this book are Z-Lon (a flashy synthetic yarn), chenille (fuzzy fibers wrapped around a thread core), tinsel, Krystal Flash (flashy metallic strands), synthetic dubbing blends, and Microfibbets, a polymer tailing material.

WAX

Dubbing wax is used to coat thread so that dubbing material adheres to it more readily. Even though most thread these days is prewaxed, a little extra wax can help, especially for beginners, who often find it hard to get the feel for twisting dubbing onto thread.

WIRE

Wire for weighting, commonly made of lead but now available in lead-free material, is wrapped around the hook shanks of some nymphs and streamers to make them sink. It is sold in gauges from extra-fine (.010) through medium (.020, 0.25) and extra large (.035). Size designations vary among manufacturers and suppliers. Note that lead wire, because it's denser, is slightly smaller in diameter than the corresponding lead-free wire. The rule of thumb for choosing weighting wire is that it should be about the same diameter as the hook you're using for the pattern.

head cement

thinner

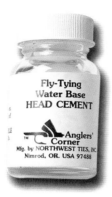

**water-based
head cement**

applicator

HEAD CEMENT

Head cement is dabbed on the head of a fly to secure the final wraps of thread. It is also used to secure materials or thread at points that tend to come loose when the fly is fished or to build up a glossy finish on the head or other parts of some flies.

As you become proficient at the whip finish, you may stop using cement to finish off the heads of your flies. But in the beginning, it's a good idea to add a dab. Use the point of your bodkin, don't use too much, and clear cement from the eye of the hook before it dries. Otherwise, you'll go crazy trying to thread a leader when you're on the stream.

Head cement should be thinned in cases where you want it to soak into the thread, as in finishing the head of a fly. Also, standard head cement thickens with time, so get a jar of thinner. Water-based head cement is handy because it requires no thinner, but it takes longer to dry. It can be stored in an applicator bottle that will help you dispense and place cement more precisely.

A PLACE TO TIE

First, your tying place must have a desk or table to which a vise can be clamped. Some table and desk tops are too thick or of the wrong shape to accept a C-clamp base. You also want a surface that's a comfortable height for working. A C-clamp vise can be raised or lowered a few inches, but not enough to make up for a desk that's way too high or low. Finally, the surface should have enough area to spread out tools and materials.

A tying area must have good light. Tying is detailed work, and it's frustrating to try to manipulate materials you can't see well. Natural light is great, and a desk by a window makes a fine daytime location. You should also have a desk lamp, preferably with a 100-watt bulb and a swing-arm or flexible neck so you can adjust it to control shadows and glare. Position the bulb above the vise and slightly to one side, so it shines down on your work without the arm of the lamp getting in your way. If you really get serious, check out the fly-tying lamps with color-corrected bulbs and infinitely adjustable necks, available from shops and catalogs.

One other tip: Thread and fibers are much more visible against a solid, medium-toned background (like the background for the photos in this book) than they are against a dark or busy background. Get a piece of gray, blue or green poster board or mat board and stand it up on your desk behind your vise.

2

Basic Techniques

The first several procedures in this chapter you will use on every fly you tie, and the others so often that they are gathered here rather than repeated in the instructions for each pattern.

Clamping a Hook in the Vise

Many fly-tying hooks are available in barbless versions. If you buy barbed hooks, smashing down the barb should be your first tying step. A barbless hook can be removed from a fish's mouth with a gentle tug, allowing you to release the fish quickly and without injury.

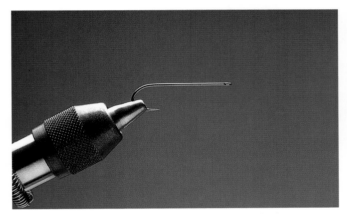

Clamp the hook in the vise at the bend with the point extending as shown. Tighten the jaws until the hook doesn't slip when you push down firmly on the eye with your finger. Don't torque down so much that you crimp the hook or damage the vise jaws. This is a matter of feel. Tighten the jaws in small increments until the hook is secure.

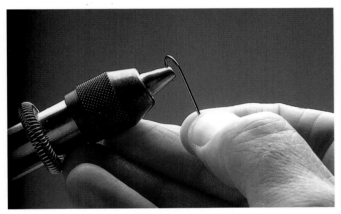

Place the hook sideways in the vise and tighten the jaws to flatten the barb. You can also do this with pliers.

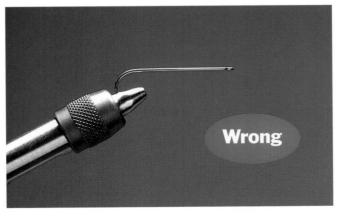

Don't bury the hook point in the jaws. This position gives you less room to work. Also, clamping down on the point of a small hook can snap it.

Load a spool of thread on your bobbin.

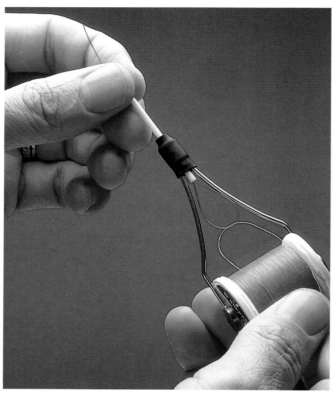

1. To thread the bobbin, stick the end of the thread through the loop in the dental floss threader, push the tip of the threader through the bobbin tube, and pull it out the other end.

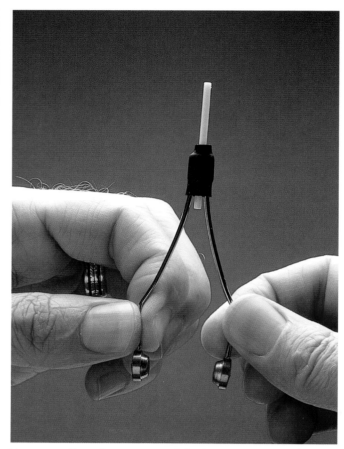

You can adjust the tension of the bobbin by stretching the arms apart (if thread comes off the spool too tightly) or pushing them together (if thread comes off too easily). Make fine adjustments after you begin tying and get a feel for the right tension. Thread should unspool when you pull on the bobbin but not so easily that you can't make snug wraps around the hook.

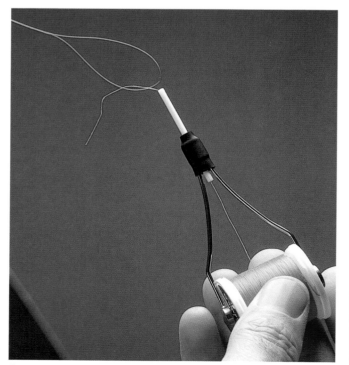

2. Pull the tip of the threader through the tube.

12

Tying instructions tell you to "tie on" when you begin a fly. This procedure isn't a knot, but a way of wrapping thread onto the shank securely enough so that it won't slip when you begin tying. It's a simple wrapping motion that will soon become automatic.

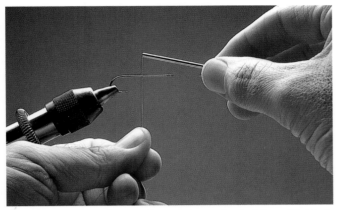
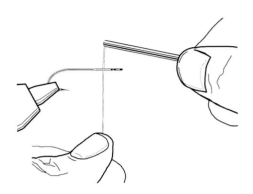

1. Pull 4 or 5 inches of thread from the bobbin. Hold the end of the thread in your left hand and the bobbin in your right on the near side of the hook.

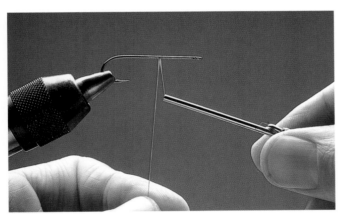
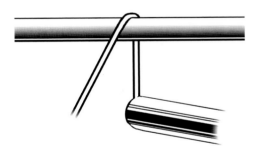

2. Wrap the bobbin once over the top of the hook, pulling the thread in either hand away from the hook as you wrap, so the wrap is snug. Note: This will be the direction of wrap for almost all tying procedures—over the top of the hook.

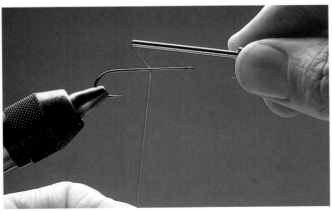
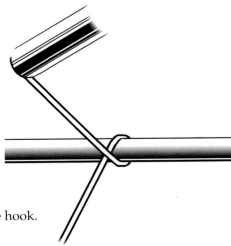

3. At the top of the next wrap, angle the bobbin toward the back of the hook.

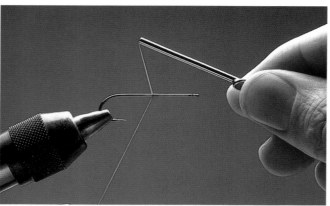

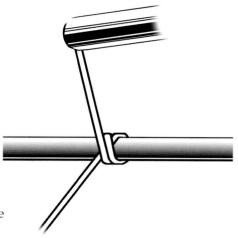

4. Directing the thread with your bottom hand toward the back of the hook, wrap 4 more times around the hook.

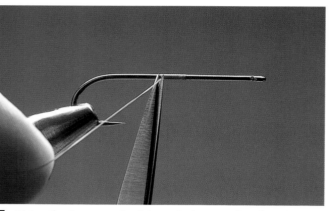

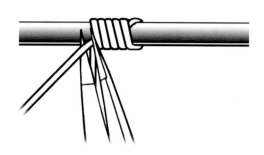

5. Trim the loose end of thread close to the shank.

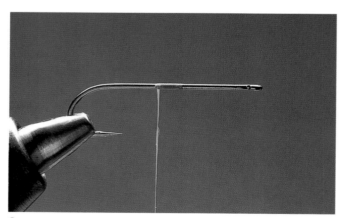

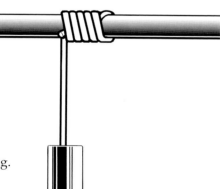

6. The thread is now secured to the hook and you're ready to begin tying.

The Right Amount of Thread

Working with the right amount of thread between bobbin and hook will make your tying easier. Adjust this amount before beginning a pattern.

Too much thread between hook and bobbin. This makes it hard to control the thread as you wrap. Reel some thread back onto the bobbin by turning the spool with your thumb and forefinger.

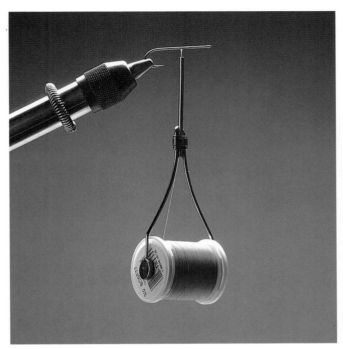

Too little thread to work with.

About the right amount of thread.

The pinch wrap (also called the essential pinch, loose wrap, or soft loop) is the standard technique for tying down hair or fibers that you want to stay together in a bundle on top of the hook. If you tie down such material without holding it in place, the bundle gets pushed all around the circumference of the hook. The trickiest part of this move is holding the material in place while sneaking the thread between the hook shank and your fingers. Repetition is the best way to get the feel for it. Put a hook in the vise. Tie on near the middle. Take a small bunch of material (any loose fibers will do) and practice the pinch wrap until you can fasten the bunch in place on top of the shank.

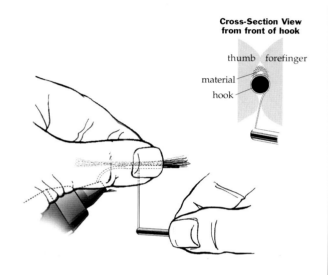

Cross-Section View
from front of hook

thumb   forefinger
material
hook

1. Hold the material in place on top of the hook by pinching it with your thumb and forefinger.

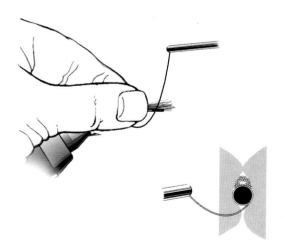

2. Lift the bobbin, guiding the thread around your thumb . . .

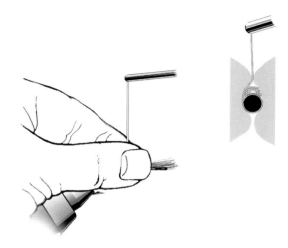

3. . . . and slipping it back between your thumb and the near side of the hook, while still pinching the material on top of the hook. It takes some practice to get the feel for this. You must bend the tip of your thumb outward enough to sneak the thread in there while maintaining pressure on the material with the pad of your thumb.

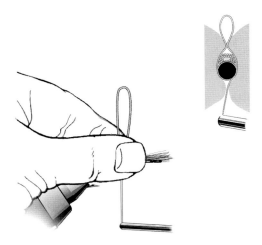

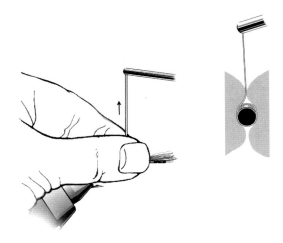

4. Loop the thread loosely over the top of the hook and slip it down between your forefinger and the far side of the hook, and pull the bobbin downward. As in Step 3, you must bend the tip of your finger out enough to admit the thread while keeping pressure on the material. The point is to hold the material in position on top of the hook while you create the loop.

6. Keep pulling up until the loop is tight around the material, and then make a few safety wraps.

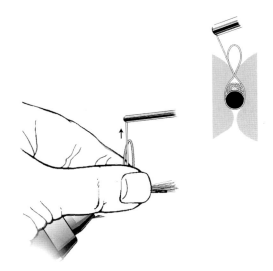

7. The material tied in place.

5. Repeat Steps 2 and 3, sneaking the thread up between your thumb and hook on the near side of the hook. Begin tightening the loop by pulling straight up. Note the diminishing loop above the tier's thumbnail as he pulls up on the bobbin.

Controlling Thread Twist

Most tying thread is flat, like ribbon, but gains a clockwise twist when wound on the spool at the factory and becomes further twisted as you wrap it around the hook. This twist is acceptable for most applications, and if you ignored all the instructions on thread twist in this book, you would still be able to tie the flies. But it's worthwhile learning the advantages of flat thread.

Flat thread is easier to control because it's limp. You can place a slack loop of flat thread exactly where you want it, whereas a loop of twisted thread will kink because of its inherent tendency to unwind when not under tension. Flat thread is also better when you don't want to build up bulk or when you need a smooth base for overlaying materials such as floss or tinsel. And finally, it's better as a base for a dubbing strand (see page 26).

Twisted thread has advantages too. Because it's circular in cross section, adjacent wraps create a ridged base that keeps materials on top from slipping back and forth. Twisted thread also has more bite than flat thread: it will dig down into stiff hair to make it flare and will bind such material tightly to the hook. By controlling the direction of twist (clockwise or counterclockwise), you can even make twisted thread push material one way or the other as you wind it around the hook.

It's very simple to alter thread twist with your bobbin hanging from the hook. To remove twist, spin the bobbin counterclockwise (when looking down on it from above) until the thread is flat. To add twist, spin the bobbin clockwise (unless otherwise directed) until the thread is twisted like a rope.

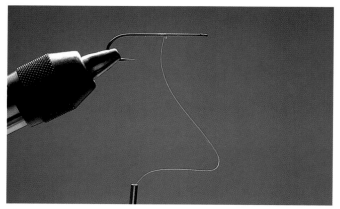

Thread with a clockwise twist, as most thread comes from the factory, will loop to the right (or even kink in that direction) when you raise the bobbin.

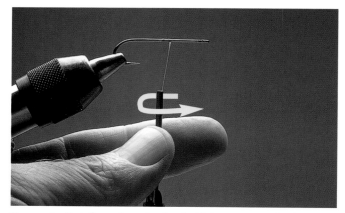

To create flat thread, spin the bobbin counterclockwise (when looking down on the bobbin from above). There is no set number of turns that will accomplish this, because threads vary in the amount of inherent twist. But if you look closely at the thread at the shank, you can see when it is flattened.

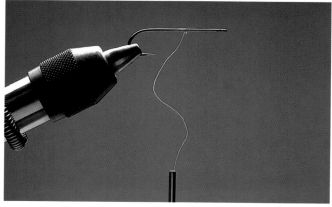

Thread with a counterclockwise twist will loop to the left when you raise the bobbin.

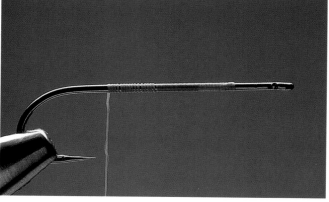

A comparison of flat (right) and twisted thread wrapped on a hook shank. Note the lower, smoother profile of the flat-thread wraps.

The flat-thread loop is a simple way of fastening material down on top of a hook.

It's used in similar situations as the pinch wrap, but it doesn't require you to trap the thread between hook and finger while pinching the material. Instead, you can pinch the material in place behind the tie-in point and make your loop in front of this point.

There are times when you must use the pinch wrap, such as with bundles of feathers or hair that would be pushed all around the shank if you didn't hold them in place while you formed your loop. But the flat-thread loop is simpler to perform than the pinch wrap.

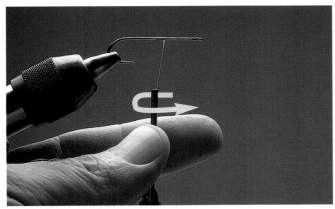

1. Spin the bobbin counterclockwise to remove twist and create flat thread.

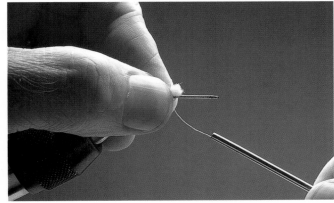

3. Loop the thread over the top of the material and up under the hook shank.

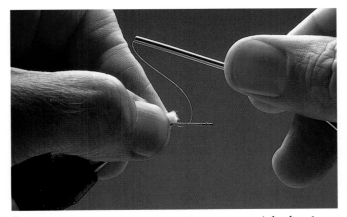

2. Hold the material to be tied in on top of the hook shank with your left hand and lift the thread over the near side of the hook with your right. Notice that the thread above the hook in this photo, even with no tension on it, is in a relaxed, manageable curve. If you try this move without first untwisting the thread, the loop will kink.

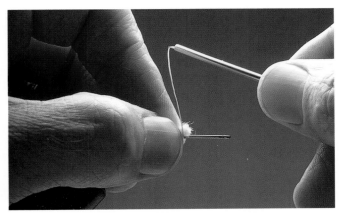

4. Pull up on the thread to cinch down the material on top of the shank.

The whip finish is the standard knot for finishing a fly. It locks the thread in place so securely that in most cases, no cement is needed. (Many experts prefer to whip finish by hand because they can tie the knot faster and with more control. The best way to learn this method is by watching someone do it.)

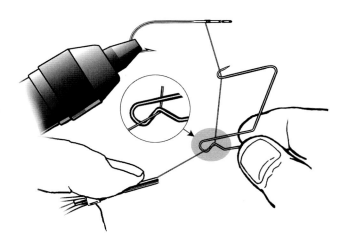

1. Begin with the bobbin about 4 or 5 inches below the hook. Gripping the tool with your forefinger behind it, so the upper shaft doesn't rotate in the handle, catch the thread in the hook at the top of the tool and lead it over the notch in the bottom.

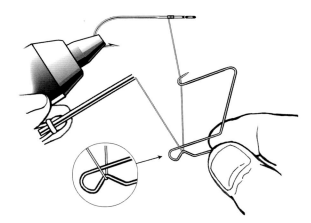

2. Raise the bobbin up and to the left, maintaining tension to keep the thread in the notch.

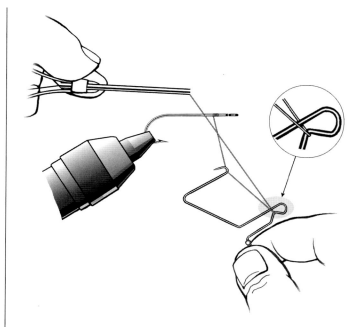

3. While continuing to raise the bobbin, drop your forefinger from behind the tool and let the tool rotate naturally in its handle. The tool flips quickly during this move, and keeping the thread in the notch is the trickiest move in the whole whip finish sequence. Once you get the feel for this step, the rest is easy. You have created a triangle of thread that you will then simply spin around the hook toward the eye.

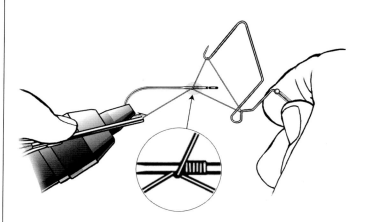

4. Spin the tool in small circles, wrapping the thread around the hook toward the eye.

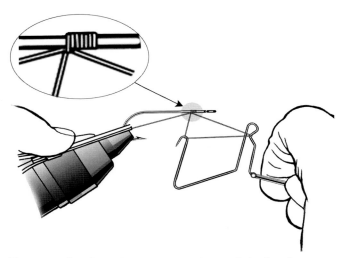

5. Wrap the thread 3 or 4 times around the hook.

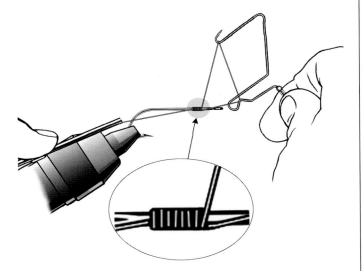

6. Disengage the thread from the notch by lifting the hook-end of the tool up . . .

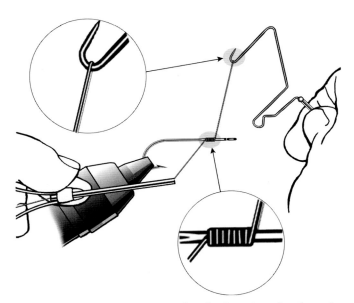

7. . . . and pulling back on the shaft to free the thread from the notch.

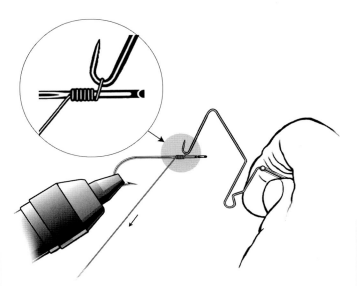

8. Pull the bobbin down to tighten the thread to the hook shank.

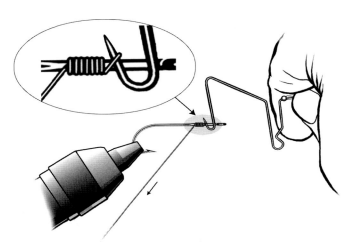

9. Maintaining downward tension on the bobbin, remove the tool and pull the thread tight.

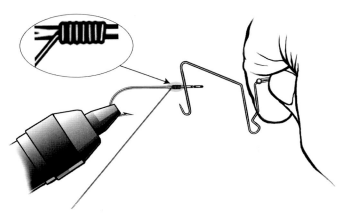

10. The completed whip finish, ready for trimming.

Repairing Broken Thread

You will occasionally break the thread while tying a pattern. If this happens at the beginning of a pattern, just undo what you've done and start over. But if you're farther along in the pattern, it will be less work to repair the thread and keep going.

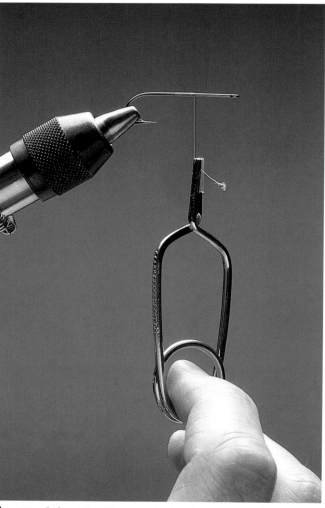

1. Attach hackle pliers to the broken end of thread and let the pliers hang.

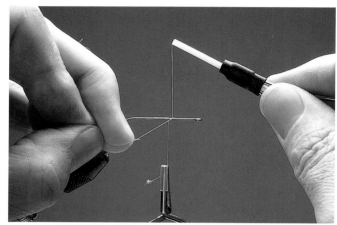

2. Tie in forward of the break.

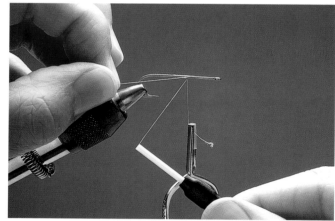

3. Holding the new tag end of thread to the left with your left hand, wrap over the shank and come up under the shank on the back (left) side of the broken thread.

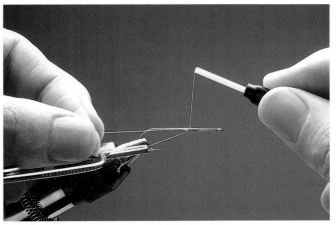

4. Holding both the hackle pliers and new tag of thread out of the way with your left hand, wind the bobbin over the old thread 3 times.

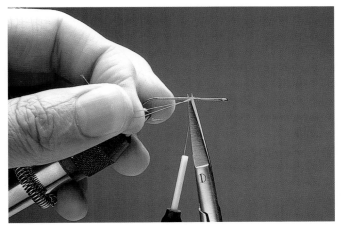

5. Trim the tag end of the new thread and the broken piece, and you're ready to continue with the pattern.

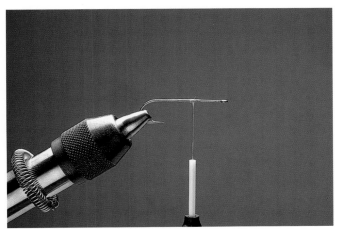

6. The repaired thread.

Dubbing

Dubbing is fur, hair, or synthetic fiber affixed to the tying thread and wrapped around the hook to form the body of a fly. Because aquatic insect bodies are not uniform in color or texture, dubbing is usually a blend of different types of fibers, either a mix of different fur types from one natural source or a blend of synthetic and natural material. Dubbing material varies in texture according to the body of the insect the fly is imitating, from the fine material often used for dry flies, to the coarse "buggy" fibers used for many nymphs.

Blending by Hand

When you need to blend a small amount of natural dubbing—say for one or two flies—you can do it by hand.

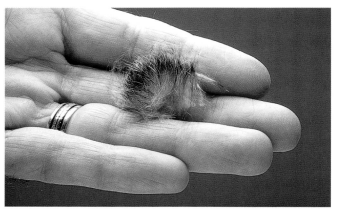

1. Cut a bunch of hair from a hide, in this case a hare's mask, making sure to get a mixture of long and short hairs of various colors.

2. Pull the hairs apart with your fingers and mix them up.

3. The hand-blended dubbing.

Blending Synthetic and Natural Materials

Preblended dubbing mixes are available in several colors. However, blending your own dubbing lets you match the insects you find in local waters and create pattern variations that may be more effective than those tied with commercial blends. Here is a general formula for blending natural and synthetic material.

Natural muskrat fur (left) and Antron fibers.

1. Before blending, chop up the Antron fibers (about one-third the total amount of material to be prepared) with scissors, so the fibers are various lengths, as shown here.

2. Cut a bunch of muskrat fur from the hide and chop about two-thirds the total amount into various lengths with scissors. Blend this chopped fur with the remaining one-third of full-length fur.

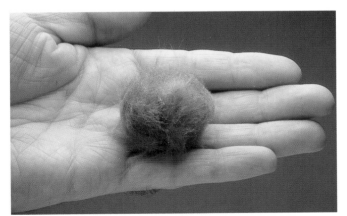

3. Blend the two materials thoroughly with your fingers until the mix looks like this. Note how the Antron fibers add sparkling highlights to the natural color of the muskrat.

Blending in a Coffee Grinder

If you're blending a larger amount of dubbing and want a more thorough mix of fibers than you can get by hand, a coffee grinder is fast and convenient.

Place a clump of dubbing material in the grinder, put the lid on, and then blend by tapping the switch 5 or 6 times, leaving it on for just a second each time.

The blended dubbing.

Comparison of hare's mask dubbing blended by hand (right) and in a coffee grinder.

Single-Thread Dubbing

There are several techniques for applying dubbing to a fly, some involving tools. But all methods involve affixing material to the thread hanging from the hook and then wrapping this dubbed thread around the shank. The single-thread method shown here is the simplest.

First you must form a dubbing strand by twisting a wisp of material around the thread hanging from the hook. This doesn't involve much dexterity, but it does require a feel for twisting the material onto the thread. Here are the key points:

- Use less material than you think you'll need. The most common beginner mistake is putting too much material on the thread, which results in a thick, lumpy body.
- Take the twist out of the thread before forming the strand (see page 18). Dubbing material adheres more readily to flat thread and is easier to slide up and down once it's on.
- Twist the dubbing onto the thread in one direction only, not back and forth. Twisting it clockwise (looking down from above) will keep the strand tight as you wind it.
- Use prewaxed thread. Some tiers find that adding a little wax to the thread helps the dubbing adhere. Simply apply a slight bit of wax to your fingers from the stick and twist it on to the length of thread hanging from the hook.

1. Eyeball the amount of dubbing material you'll need for the body of the fly. Remember that you'll need less than you think, so estimate on the sparse side.

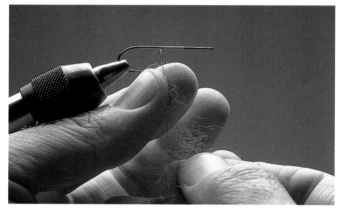

2. Holding the material loosely against the thread with your lower hand, begin twisting the material clockwise onto the thread with the thumb and forefinger of your upper hand. Don't twist the material back and forth; it won't stay on the thread. Twist in one direction only.

3. Work down, pressing material onto the thread with a light twisting motion.

4. The finished dubbing strand. Note the short bit of bare thread next to the hook. You can take this up by winding it around the shank. Or, you can slide the strand up next to the shank before you begin wrapping.

If you try to slide the dubbing strand up the thread by pinching it with your thumb and forefinger, you may separate the strand.

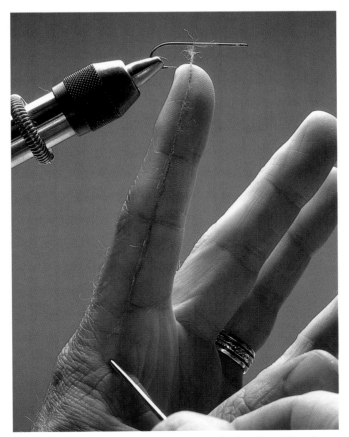

5. A better way to slide it up is with the flat side of your finger against the whole length of the strand.

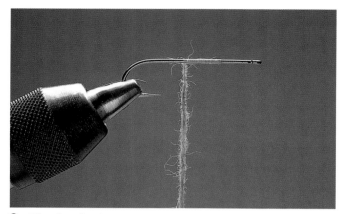

6. The finished strand, ready to be wrapped around the hook.

9. The completed body. (If you were tying a fly, at this point you would strip the excess dubbing from the thread hanging from the hook and continue with the pattern.) Note that the contour of the body is smooth, not lumpy. This is a result of material applied evenly to the thread before wrapping. Note also the wisps of material sticking up that give the body a "buggy" look, a desired feature of many fly bodies.

7. Wind the dubbed thread (in this case forward, toward the eye) around the shank in over-and-under, adjacent wraps . . .

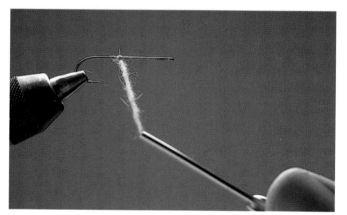

8. . . . keeping enough tension on the thread to make snug wraps.

3

Woolly Bugger

Tail · Body · Hackle

The Woolly Bugger was created in 1967 by Russell Blessing of Lancaster, Pennsylvania, who tied a marabou tail onto a Woolly Worm in an attempt to imitate a hellgrammite. It's an ideal first fly—large, easy to tie, and deadly on fish everywhere. Depending on the body of water, fish may take it for a leech, a sculpin, a large nymph, or a crayfish. The buggy hackle and the undulating action of the marabou tail are irresistible.

Cast a Woolly Bugger across and slightly upstream. Let the fly drift until your line is straight downstream, and then twitch it back to you along the bottom. In a lake, let it sink to the bottom and then retrieve slowly.

Thread · Hook · Wire · Marabou · Chenille · Rooster saddle

Hook Streamer, 4X long, size 4–12.

Daiichi 1750, Mustad 9674, Tiemco 9395.

Weight Medium-gauge wire.

Thread Black 6/0.

Tail Black marabou plume or blood feather.

The short, fluffy feathers called marabou, originally from African storks, now come from domestic turkeys. They are dyed a number of colors. Two types of marabou feathers are sold: plumes and bloods (or "fluffs"). The plume is the longer. A full, fluffy blood feather is most convenient for making this tail, but you can use the fluffy end of a plume as well. Avoid stringy feathers; they don't wave and undulate as much in the water.

Body Olive chenille, medium.

Hackle Black saddle hackle.

Many color variations are used, including grizzly and brown. Choose a saddle that has feathers with soft, wide center webs.

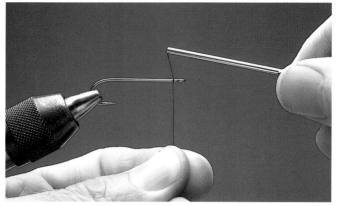

1. Tie on, starting 1 to 2 eye-lengths behind the eye of the hook. (See pages 13–14 for tying on.)

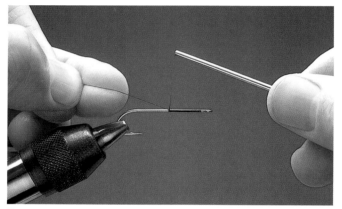

2. Wrap the thread rearward in adjacent wraps, laying it over the tag end held taut to the rear with your left hand. Note the slight upward angle at which this tag end is held to the left. This forces each wrap to slide down neatly into place next to the previous one.

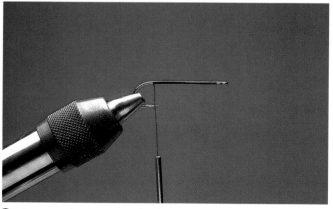

3. Stop at the bend of the hook and trim off excess thread as close as you can to the hook. You have now laid a thread base over which you will apply weighting wire.

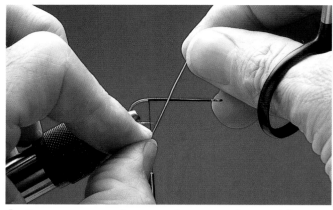

4. Start wrapping the wire about two-thirds of the shank-length back from the eye. Wind it forward over the top of the hook in tight adjacent wraps, stopping well short of the eye. (See Step 7 for the length of the completed wrap.) Note how the tier wears the scissors slid back on his thumb and finger when he's not using them.

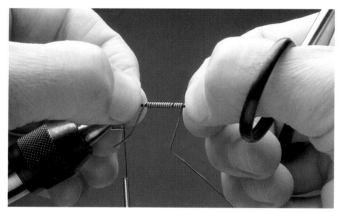

5. Push from either end with your thumbnails to tighten up the wraps.

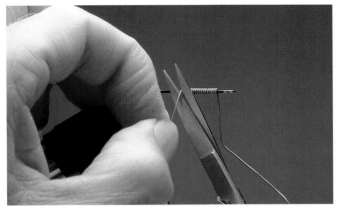

6. Trim both ends of the wire as close to the shank as possible. Don't use the very tips of your good scissors for trimming wire; it will dull them for fine work. Cut the wire farther down in the blades, or use another pair of scissors or toenail clippers for wire and coarse material.

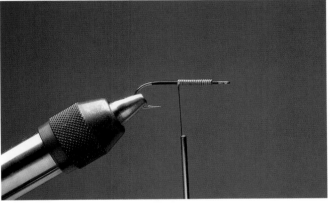

7. The completed wire wraps. You want a smooth, snag-free base over which to continue tying. If either end of the wire sticks up after trimming, press it against the hook with your fingernail.

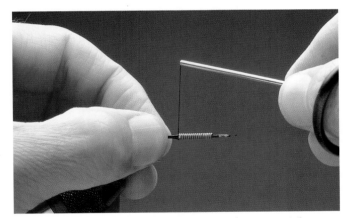

8. Build up a tapered thread base at the rear of the wire. Start by winding flat thread back a few wraps from where it's hanging in Step 7, then go forward, wrapping the thread over itself 20 times or more until the thread base is almost the same diameter as the wire base, as shown here.

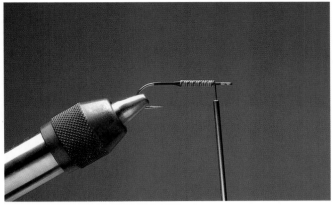

9. Wind thread forward in wide wraps over the wire base.

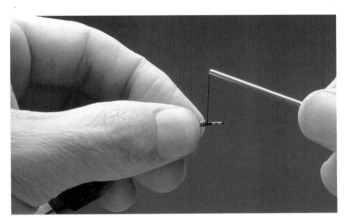

10. Build a thread base like the one in Step 8 at the front of the wire.

11. Wrap back to the end of the wire and let the bobbin hang.

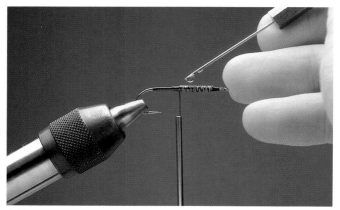

12. Apply a thin bead of head cement along the top length of the wire.

Pause for a moment while the cement dries and look at what you've done: built a tight base on which to tie the rest of the fly. Loosely applied weighting wire will slip back and forth and rotate around the shank, pulling the fly apart as you fish it. Building up a thread dam at front and back, winding over the wire, and adding head cement all help lock the wire in position and create a fly that will stay together through a season of fishing.

13. Select a marabou blood feather for a tail. It should have thick, even, fluffy ends.

14. Strip the barbs from the base of the feather with your fingers, leaving a feather at least twice as long as the hook.

15. The prepared feather.

16. The tail should be 1 hook-shank in length. To measure this, hold the feather on top of the shank and adjust your grip so that when your thumbnail is at the eye, the tips of the tail are directly above the bend of the hook.

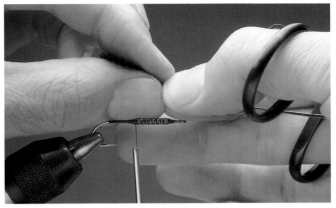

17. Transfer the tail to your left hand, pinching it at the spot you were holding it with your right.

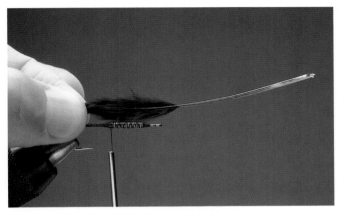

18. Hold the feather on top of the hook with your left thumbnail directly above the bend. The amount of feather to the left of your thumbnail is what will extend from the end of the fly.

19. Trim the feather at a point directly above the bobbin tube, which in this case is $1/4$ inch forward (toward the eye) of where you gripped it in the previous step. This extra length will be used for tying the feather down.

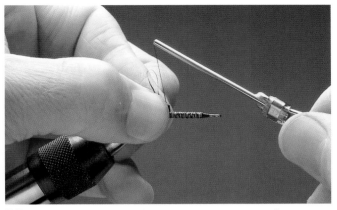

20. Tie in the base of the tail just forward of the bend with a pinch wrap (see page 16).

Here, the loop of the pinch wrap has been formed above the hook.

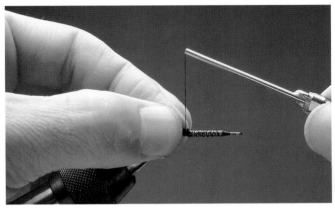

21. Tighten the loop by pulling up.

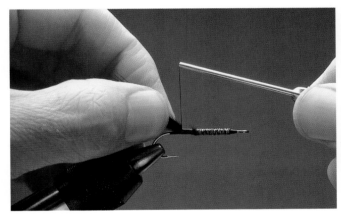

22. Holding the tail up and to the rear, wrap thread rearward, over its base.

23. Wrap back to the bend and let the bobbin hang. Take a moment to look at the completed tail. This was a good choice of feather—nice and fluffy, so it will have good action in the water—and it's tied in at just the right spot. A tail tied in forward of this spot will be too long and tend to wrap around the hook bend when you're casting and fishing. A tail tied in farther to the rear, into the bend, will slant downward, not straight out like this one. Don't be discouraged if your first Woolly Bugger tail isn't perfect. If the proportions are about right and it doesn't fall off the hook, the fly will catch fish.

24. Cut a 3- or 4-inch length of chenille and strip some fuzz from one end with your fingers to expose about $^1/_8$-inch of the core.

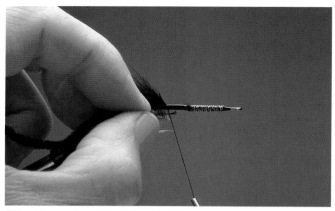

25. Tie in the chenille at the base of the tail: hold the exposed core beneath the hook and wrap three times around it.

26. Let the chenille hang while you move on to the hackle.

27. Choose a hackle feather with a wide center web.

Woolly Bugger

28. The hackle barbs should be about 1¹/₂ to 2 times as long as the width of the hook gap.

Measure this by bending the stem of the hackle into a circle and holding the barbs against the hook. Note: You'll be tying in this feather at its tip, which is at the far right above. (You can lay the chenille on top of the vise for now, to keep it out of the way.)

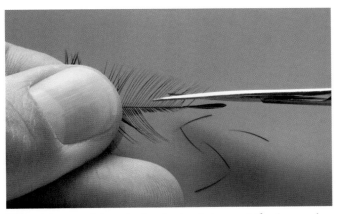

29. After stroking the barbs back toward the base of the feather so they stick out at right angles from the stem, trim them off the last ¹/₂-inch of stem. This creates a place to tie in the hackle.

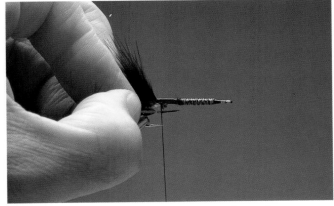

30. Holding back the longer barbs behind the tie-in spot with your thumb and forefinger, position the trimmed hackle tip alongside the hook slightly in front of the place you tied in the chenille.

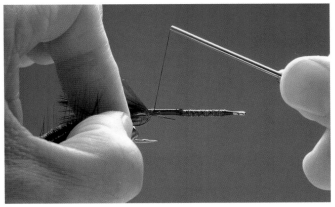

31. Tie in the hackle with 6 tight, adjacent wraps along the length of the prepared tip, and let the feather hang there. The tip must be securely attached so it doesn't pull free when you later begin wrapping the hackle around the shank.

32. Wrap the thread forward to an eye-length behind the eye and let the bobbin hang.

33. Holding the hackle toward the front with your right hand, wind the chenille once around the shank behind the hackle feather.

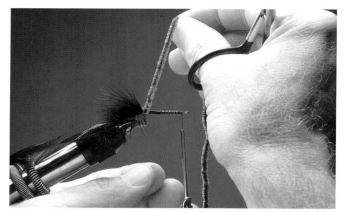

34. Now move the hanging hackle feather to the rear, out of your way (the tier above has fastened it to a materials clip on his vise, a handy accessory), and continue wrapping the chenille forward in tightly adjacents wraps, going over the hook with your right hand . . .

35. . . . catching the chenille underneath with your left . . .

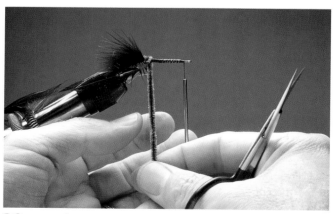

36. . . . while moving your right hand around the bobbin to pick up the chenille for the next wind. (This hand-swapping lets you navigate around the hanging bobbin as you wind.)

37. Wind the chenille forward to where the thread is hanging, stopping at least 1 eye-length short of the eye. Holding the chenille to the right, pick up the bobbin in your left hand and wrap the thread 3 or 4 times tightly around the chenille to secure it. (You'll have to let go of the bobbin as you pass it over the hook.)

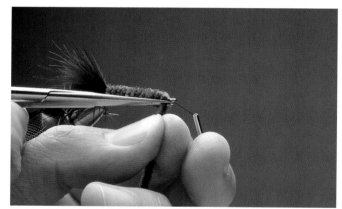

38. Trim the excess chenille and let the bobbin hang there.

39. Grasp the hackle feather by its free end and wind it forward snugly over the chenille in even spirals. With the fingers of your left hand, stroke the barbs rearward as you go, so they point toward the back of the fly, as in the next photo.

40. When you've wrapped the hackle to the front, hold it firmly in place with your right hand and strip the fibers from both sides of the stem to create a tie-in place.

41. Tie down the hackle with 3 tight, adjacent wraps of thread. Because hackle stems are springy and smooth, they tend to unwind if not tightly secured. Adjacent wraps are more secure than those made right on top of each other.

42. Trim the excess hackle from around the eye, whip finish, and add a drop of head cement.

This is how the finished head should look. Note that the hackle is well back from the eye.

43. Woolly Bugger.

Look at the proportions of the finished fly: The tail is about as long as the hook shank (eye to bend), and the hackle barbs sticking out from the hook shank are $1^1/2$ to 2 times as long as the width of the hook gap. Notice also how the hackle is swept to the rear, and how the tail is even, fluffy and in line with the hook, not pointing up or down.

Your first fly may not look exactly like this. Even among professional tiers there's a lot of variation in Woolly Buggers. And keep in mind that the fish don't care all that much about neatness.

4

Gold-Ribbed Hare's Ear

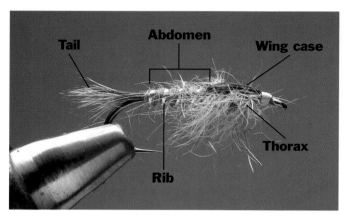

Tail — Abdomen — Wing case — Thorax — Rib

The Gold-Ribbed Hare's Ear remains the best-selling nymph pattern in America for the simple reason that it catches a lot of trout. Its rough, buggy body with the subtle blend of color imitates a number of insect forms on the bottom of the stream, including mayfly nymphs.

Cast it upstream and let it drift naturally on or near the bottom. Add a small split shot to your leader in faster or deeper water. If you have trouble detecting the soft takes of trout, attach a strike indicator (a small foam press-on disc, available at fly shops) to your leader at least twice the depth of the water up from the fly, and watch it closely. When the indicator twitches, set the hook.

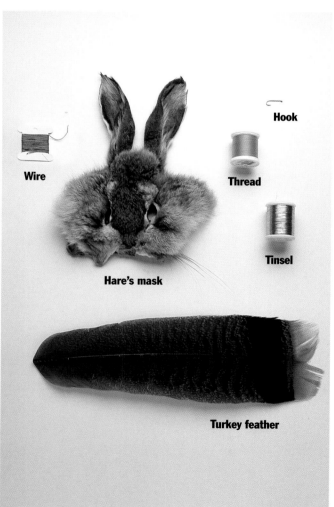

Wire — Hare's mask — Hook — Thread — Tinsel — Turkey feather

Hook	Standard nymph, size 10–16.
	Daiichi 1560, Mustad 3906B, Tiemco 3761.
Weight	Fine-gauge wire (optional).
Thread	Tan 6/0.
Tail	Guard hair from hare's mask.
	"Hare's mask" refers to the hair and fur around the face, including the ears, of a European hare. The mask consists of several types of hair of different length, stiffness, and color. The guard hairs are long and stiff, while the fur is short and flexible. A complete hare's mask is available in a package from fly shops and catalogs, or you can buy a pre-blended mix.
Rib	Oval gold tinsel, fine.
Abdomen	Hare's mask fur blend.
Wing Case	Mottled turkey feather.
Thorax	Hare's mask fur blend.

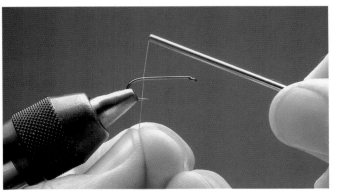

1. Tie on at the bend. Remember to use the steps on pages 13–14 whenever you tie on. (If you wish to weight the fly, tie on just behind the eye instead and proceed with steps 1–12 of the Woolly Bugger on pages 30–32.)

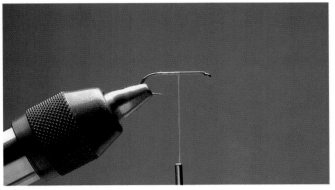

2. Wind forward to the midpoint of the shank and let the bobbin hang.

3. Snip a bunch of guard hairs (the longer, stiff hairs) from a hare's mask. Grip the tips with your fingers and snip down close to the hide.

4. This will be the tail of the fly.

5. Pick out the soft fuzz ("underfur") from the base of the fur and discard it.

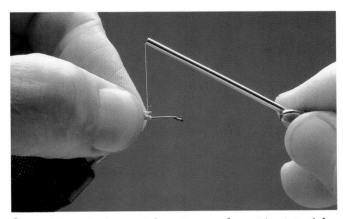

6. Holding the base of the tail over the midpoint of the hook with thumb and forefinger, tie it in there using a pinch wrap or flat thread loop. (To find the right tie-in point, look at the next step to see how much the tail should extend.)

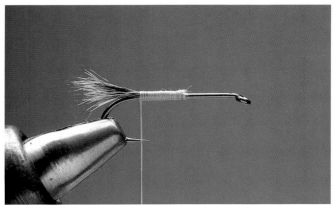

7. Holding the tail in place, wrap rearward to the bend and let the bobbin hang.

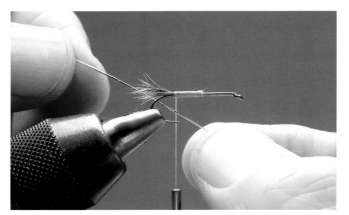

8. Cut a 3-inch length of gold oval tinsel and hold it behind the hook but in front of the thread, as shown.

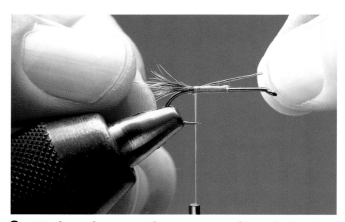

9. Lift the right end of the tinsel up behind the hook, trapping it between the hanging thread and the hook shank. (Historical note: Wayne Luallen first saw this technique used by a teenage tier named Susie Fork at a salmon fly tying demonstration in San Francisco many years ago. She was using it on floss, but Wayne has found it great for trapping a variety of materials in place for tie-in.)

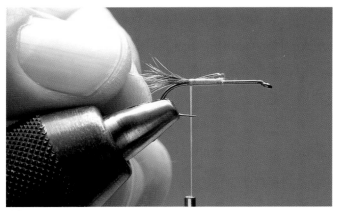

10. Tie the tinsel in at the bend and pull it rearward until the tag end extends to where the thread base begins, as shown above. Wind thread forward over the tag end and let the bobbin hang at the midpoint of the hook.

11. Cut a mixture of fur from a hare's mask and blend it according to the instructions on page 24. You will use this blend for both abdomen and thorax. Take a small amount of the blend and twist it clockwise onto the thread. (If you twist it on counterclockwise, it will tend to loosen as you wrap it forward around the shank.) This will form the abdomen of the nymph. Set aside the extra dubbing for the thorax.

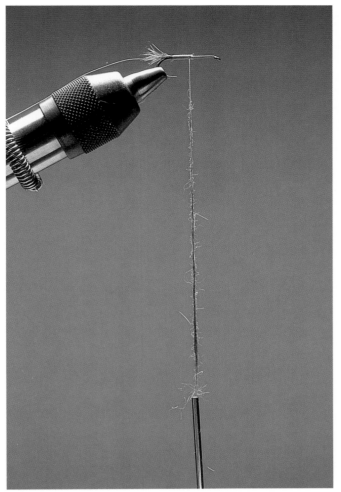

12. Put a little more material on the bottom of the dubbing strand than the top so the abdomen will be tapered when wrapped on the hook—thicker at the front (see Step 13). Note that about a shank-length of bare thread is hanging from the hook before the dubbing begins.

13. Wind rearward to the bend. This will take up the length of bare thread in the previous photo and position the top of the dubbing strand right below the hook.

14. Wind the strand forward in tight, adjacent wraps to the midpoint of the shank, and let the bobbin hang. Pick off any dubbing left on the thread. Note the front-to-rear taper of the abdomen and the untidy fibers sticking out. Both features are desirable: They make this pattern look more like the real thing.

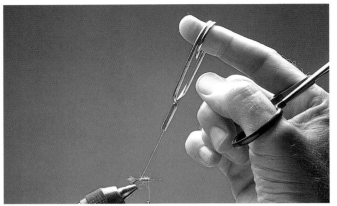

15. Grasp the end of the tinsel with hackle pliers (the tinsel being fine, it is easier to use pliers than your fingers) and begin winding it forward in diagonal wraps.

16. Continue winding the tinsel forward in diagonal wraps until you reach the front of the abdomen. Hold the extra tinsel to the right and wrap it to the hook shank with several turns of thread.

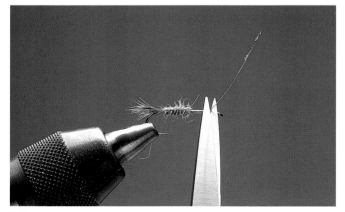

17. After you've wrapped the end of the tinsel, let the bobbin hang (it's hidden behind the scissors here) and trim off the tag end of the tinsel.

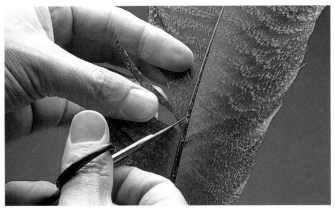

18. Cut a piece of turkey feather for the wing case. The piece should be a little narrower than the gap of the hook.

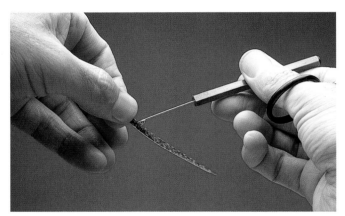

19. Put a drop of head cement on the feather . . .

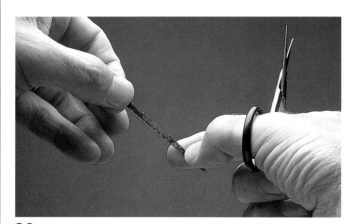

20. . . . and spread it down the length of the feather with your thumb and forefinger. This will help keep the feather together when you form the wing case.

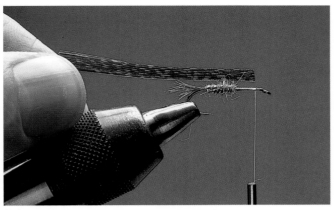

21. When the cement is dry, trim the tip square, and the feather is prepared for tie-in.

22. Position the feather, shiny side up, tip facing toward the eye, and tie it in 1 eye-length behind the eye with a few wraps of flat thread. Keep the feather flat on top of the hook, not twisted.

23. Wind back over the base of the feather to where the dubbing begins and let the bobbin hang.

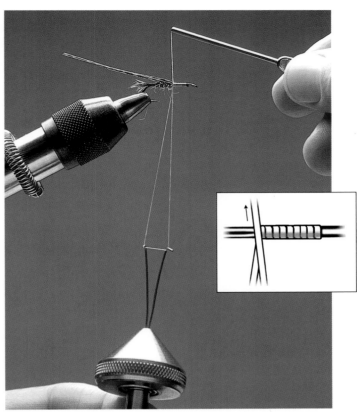

24. Pull some thread from the bobbin, loop it through the hooks of the dubbing twister, and bring the bobbin tip back up to the hook shank.

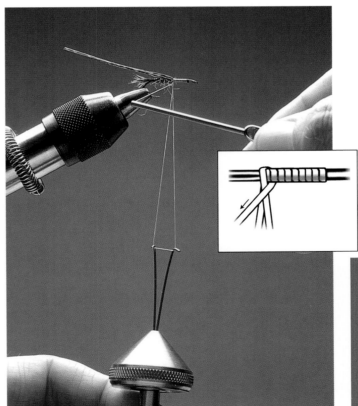

25. Don't let go of the dubbing twister with your left hand. When you've passed the bobbin over the front of the loop . . .

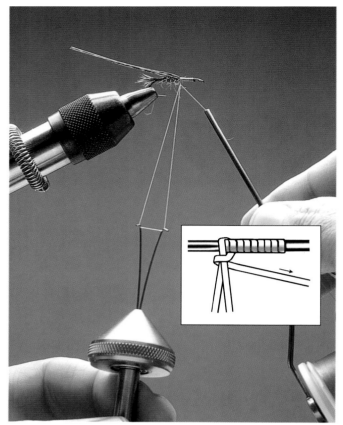

26. . . . let the bobbin go and pick it up on the back side of the loop with your right hand, completing the wrap around the two strands.

28. With the dubbing loop now locked in place at the shank, put a bit of blended hare's mask dubbing between the strands of the loop. You'll need a larger clump than you used for the abdomen because the thorax is thicker.

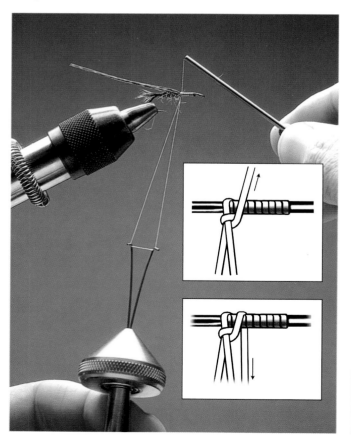

27. Wrap once more over the top of the hook.

29. Spin the dubbing twister counterclockwise to twist the material into a strand. (This counterclockwise spin makes for tighter adjacent wraps when you wind the dubbing rearward on the hook.)

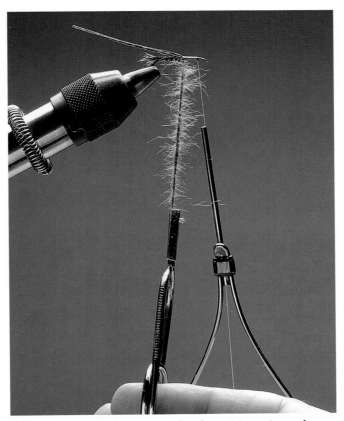

30. Remove the bottom of the thread loop from the dubbing twister and grab the tip of the strand with your hackle pliers.

31. Wind the dubbing forward.

32. Stop well short of the eye and tie off the dubbing with 3 wraps of thread. Trim excess dubbing.

33. Fold the turkey feather and pull it forward. This will be the wing case.

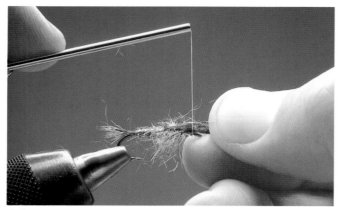

34. Tie down the forward end of the feather, just behind the eye, with 3 wraps of thread.

35. Trim the excess feather, whip finish, and add a drop of head cement.

36. Gold-Ribbed Hare's Ear.

Although the tail, abdomen, and thorax are all made from hare's mask, note how different the material looks on various parts of the fly: the thick, straight guard hairs of the tail, the tightly dubbed abdomen, and the frizzy fibers of the thorax. The scraggly, multi-hued look of the dubbing is desirable: It makes the body look more like a natural nymph.

Top view.

5

Beadhead Pheasant Tail Nymph

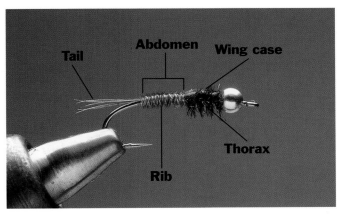

The Pheasant Tail Nymph was created in the 1950s by Frank Sawyer, a famous British tier and riverkeeper on the Avon, to imitate Baetis nymphs. He tied the pattern without thread, using fine copper wire to hold the materials on the hook. Known now to tiers as a "PT," the Pheasant Tail remains an essential nymph pattern and has been adapted by many American tiers, including Al Troth of Montana.

Beadhead versions of nymph patterns have proven very successful, probably because of their added flash and the jigging action created by the forward weight. Fish the Beadhead PT like other nymphs—cast it across stream and let it drift down, bumping along the bottom.

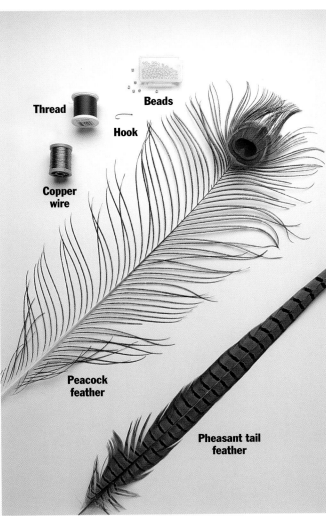

Hook	Beadhead nymph, 2X long, size 10–20.
	Daiichi 1260, Mustad C53S, Tiemco 2312.
Bead	Gold.
	Use extra small ($3/32$ inch) for hook sizes 14–20; small ($1/8$ inch) for sizes 10–12.
Thread	Rust 6/0.
Tail	Pheasant tail barbs.
	Use a ring-neck pheasant center tail feather as the source for the tail, abdomen and wing case barbs for this pattern.
Abdomen	Pheasant tail barbs.
Rib	Fine copper wire.
Wing Case	Pheasant tail barbs.
Thorax	Peacock herl.

Note: Tan thread is used here because it shows up better in the photos. Use the rust thread specified in the recipe to tie your fly.

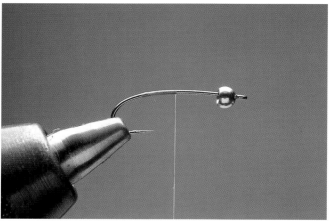

1. Smash down the barb and thread a bead onto the hook, starting the point through the smaller hole. (Most fly-tying beads have one hole larger than the other.) Tie on at the bend of the hook and wrap forward to the midpoint.

2. Pull 4 or 5 barbs from a pheasant tail feather, as shown, and cut them from the main stem.

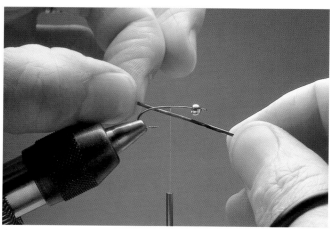

3. Position the tail barbs underneath the hook and in front of the thread, as shown, and then lift the left end of the barbs under and behind the hook, as you did with the tinsel in Step 9 on page 40.

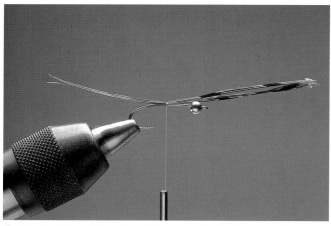

4. Tie in the tail at the midpoint of the hook with 3 wraps of thread.

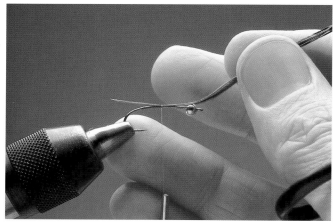

5. Lift the butt end of the tail up and pull it forward until the tail is the right length, extending slightly beyond the bend, as shown. If you don't lift up as you pull, the thread will also be pulled forward.

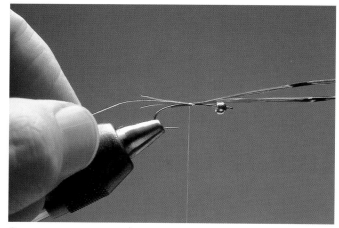

6. Cut a 3-inch length of copper wire and tie it in on the near side of the hook at the same place you tied in the tail. After tying in, slide the wire into place under the thread wraps by pulling it gently rearward until it is in the position shown here.

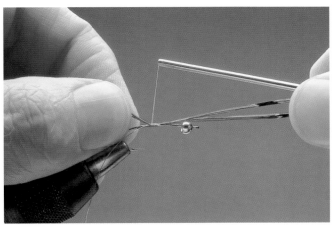

7. Making sure thread is flat (spin the bobbin if necessary—see page 18), lift the tail and wind rearward over the wire and tail.

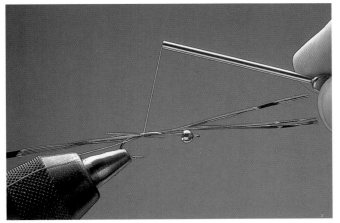

8. Cut another 4 or 5 barbs from the pheasant feather and tie them in at the bend, tips extending forward to mid-shank. These will be used to form the abdomen of the nymph.

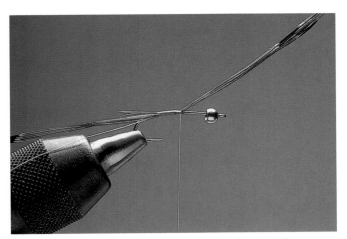

9. Wrap thread forward to secure the base of the abdomen barbs, then let the bobbin hang.

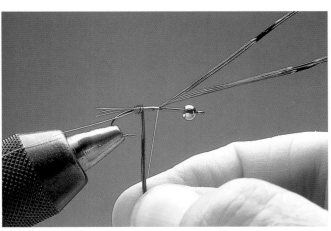

10. Grasp the abdomen barbs (those extending past the rear of the hook) by the butts and wind them forward around the shank.

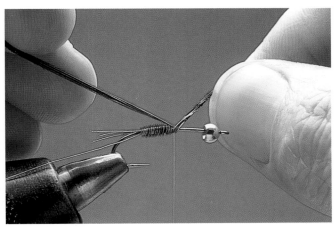

11. When you reach the wing case barbs, pull them rearward with your left hand and wrap the abdomen barbs once in front of them.

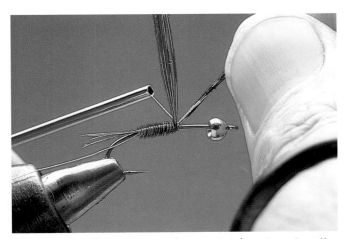

12. Pick up the bobbin with your left hand, and, still holding the abdomen barbs to the right, make 2 wraps of thread between abdomen and wing case.

49

13. Leave the excess abdomen barbs standing where they are. They will become part of the wing case.

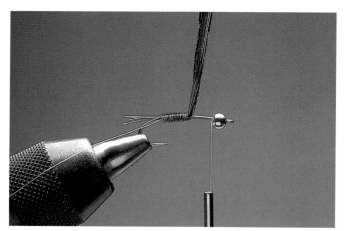

14. Wind the thread forward to the bead.

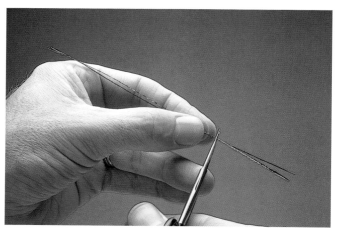

15. Pull a few barbs (or "herl," as peacock barbs are known) from a peacock feather and trim off the brittle butt sections, leaving a strand about 4 inches long.

16. Tie the butt ends of herl in behind the bead with 3 wraps of thread and, holding the herl to the rear against the hook, wrap thread rearward over it, stopping at the start of the abdomen.

17. Wrap thread forward to the bead and let the bobbin hang.

18. Wind the herl forward to the bead.

19. Tie down the herl with 3 wraps of thread and trim off the excess. Let the bobbin hang there.

20. Grasp the wire that you left hanging at the rear of the hook and wind it forward, but in reverse direction than usual—first *under* the hook on the near side and then over the top toward you. Winding in the opposite direction in which the abdomen barbs were wound locks the barbs in place. If you wrap both wire and barbs forward in the same direction around the hook, the barbs are more likely to unravel when a fish strikes.

21. Continue winding the wire forward in evenly spaced, diagonal wraps, around the wing case and over the herl.

22. When you reach the bead, tie down the wire with 2 wraps of thread and then cut or break it off close to the shank.

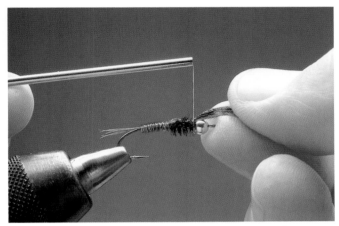

23. Bend the wing case barbs forward, wrap them in place with 3 wraps of thread, trim the excess, and whip finish.

24. Beadhead Pheasant Tail Nymph.

Note how the green highlights in the peacock herl catch the light. This is thought to be a key feature in the fly's appeal to trout. Note also the spacing of the spirals of wire around the body.

6

Elk Hair Caddis

Wing

Body

Rib

Hackle

Montana guide Al Troth created the Elk Hair Caddis to imitate a tan sedge, a caddisfly found in abundance on the riffles of freestone streams everywhere. The pattern is unique in that the wire ribbing is wound through the hackle, securing and reinforcing it in its slant-back position.

The fly is most effective when fished in fast water, where caddis naturally occur. Its light color and high-riding profile make it easy to follow through choppy water.

Hook	Dry fly, 1X or 2X short, size 12–18.
	Daiichi 1310, Mustad 94838 or R48, Tiemco 921.
Thread	Tan 6/0.
Rib	Fine gold wire.
Body	Hare's mask blend.
	The same dubbing blend as for the Gold-Ribbed Hare's Ear will work for this fly.
Hackle	Ginger or tan dry fly hackle.
Wing	Light elk hair or bleached deer hair.
	A lice comb or an electric razor brush is handy for removing the underfur from deer and elk hair.

Hook

Thread

Gold wire

Light elk hair

Hare's mask blend

Ginger rooster cape

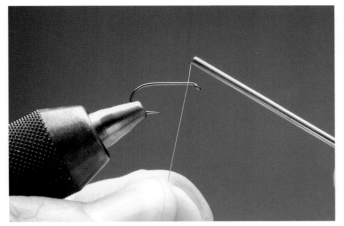

1. Tie on about 2 eye-lengths behind the eye.

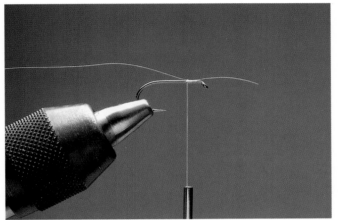

2. Wrap thread about ¹/₃ the way back the shank and tie in a 3-inch length of gold wire on the far side of the hook with a few wraps, leaving about a ¹/₂-inch tag end at the front.

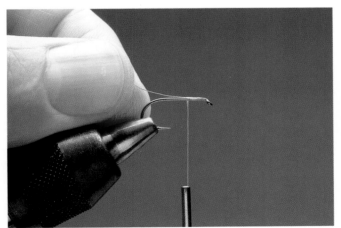

3. Pull the wire gently rearward to slide the tag end underneath the thread base. The wire is now secure and you have a smooth base over which to continue tying.

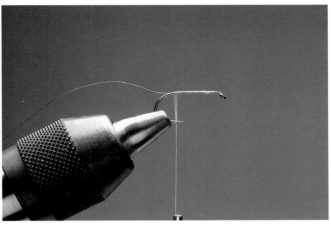

4. Wind thread back to the bend, over the wire. Spin the bobbin so the thread is flat (see page 18).

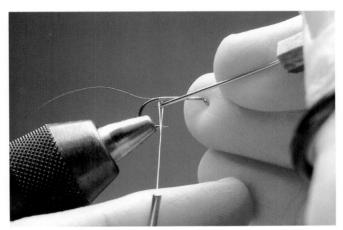

5. Poke your bodkin through the center of the thread, separating it. Note: The split-thread dubbing method shown here is an alternative to the single-thread method shown previously. It is a simple, quick way to dub a body without building up much bulk. The only disadvantage is that split thread is weaker than a whole strand. If you prefer, you can dub this fly with the single-strand method.

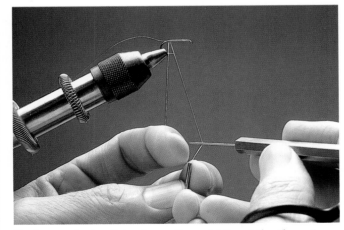

6. Draw the bodkin down the middle of the thread about 2 inches, splitting it in half.

7. Take a sparse bit of blended hare's mask dubbing (see page 24), pull it into a strip as long as the split thread, and fit it loosely between the strands of thread.

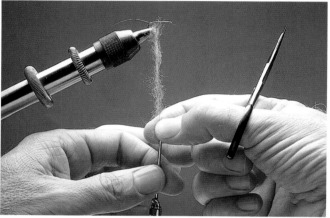

8. Twist the barrel of the bobbin counterclockwise until you have formed a strand of dubbing like the one in the next photo.

9. The twisted dubbing, ready to wind.

10. Wind the dubbing forward in snug, adjacent wraps to a few eye-lengths behind the eye.

11. You will probably end up with a length of unused dubbing, as above. Spin the bobbin clockwise to loosen the strand, and then pick the material off the thread with your fingers.

12. When the thread is stripped of excess dubbing, as above, make a few wraps of flat thread toward the eye to lay a base on which to tie in the hackle feather.

13. Select a hackle feather with barbs no longer than $1^1/_2$ times the width of the hook gap. Measure this by curling the feather next to the hook gap, as in Step 28 (page 35) of the Woolly Bugger.

14. Strip the webby barbs—in this case, the central black fibers toward the base—and fuzz off the base of the stem and trim it, leaving about $^1/_8$ inch of bare stem. The photo above shows the prepared hackle feather.

15. Tie in the stem of the hackle feather, shiny side up, with 3 tight wraps of thread. (Hackle feathers have a dull and a shiny side, which will be apparent if you flip the feather back and forth in good light.)

16. Grasp the tip of the hackle feather with hackle pliers.

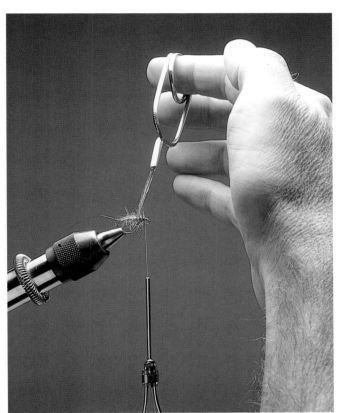

17. Wind the hackle feather rearward to the bend, passing the pliers over the hook with your right hand and picking them up underneath with your left.

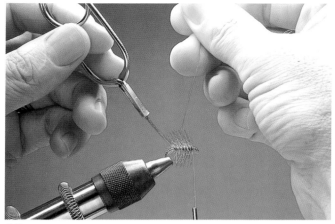

18. When you reach the bend, pass the pliers from your right hand to your left, maintaining enough upward tension to keep the hackle from unraveling. While holding the hackle pliers up, tie down the hackle at the bend with 2 tight, adjacent wraps of wire.

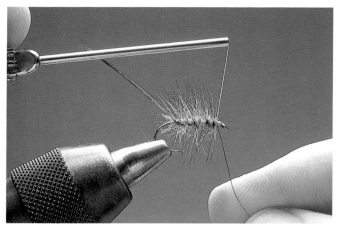

21. Wind the wire forward to just behind the eye. Holding the tag end of the wire down and to the right, pick up the bobbin with your left hand and tie off the wire with a few wraps.

19. Begin winding the wire forward, wiggling the wire side-to-side as you go to fit the wire down *between* the hackle barbs rather than wrapping over them and pinning them down to the shank.

22. Trim the excess wire close against the shank by breaking it off with your fingers or slicing it with the middle of your scissors blades.

20. After the first few wraps of wire, the hackle is locked in place on the shank. You can now unhook the hackle pliers and continue winding the wire forward, moving it side-to-side to avoid pinning down the hackle barbs.

23. Cut off the excess hackle feather.

24. Trim the top of the hackle level with the hook shank so the wing will lie flat on top.

25. The trimmed hackle.

26. Cut a bunch of elk hair about a ¹/₂-inch wide from the hide. See Step 27 to get an idea of the size of this bunch, which will be used to make the wing. For your first fly, it's better to cut a little more than you think you'll need. You can always discard the extra.

27. Clean the underfur from the butts of the fibers with an electric razor brush or a fine-toothed comb.

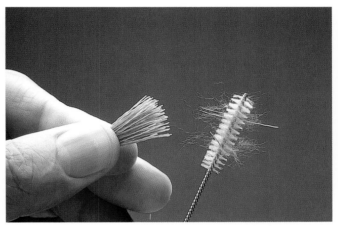

28. Notice how the butts are now free of underfur. Hair that has been combed like this stacks more easily.

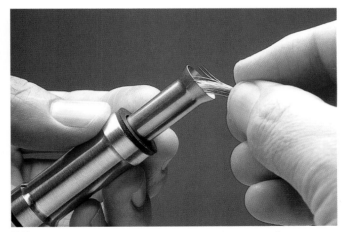

29. Place the hair in the stacker, tips first. (The tips are the finely pointed ends of the hair; the butts are the ends toward the hide, as shown in Step 26.) If you inspect the clump before you put it in the stacker, you'll see that the tips are uneven, as they occur on the animal. The purpose of the stacker is to align the tips so you can create a wing with an even edge.

30. Tap the hair stacker on the table 2 or 3 times. This forces the tips to the bottom of the cylinder. Tapping at an angle makes them align more neatly.

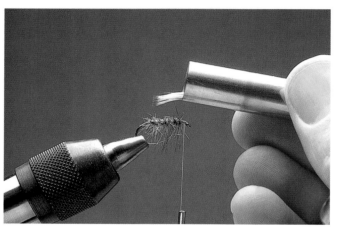

31. Holding the stacker level with your right hand, slowly remove the cap. The aligned tips will stick out the end. With your left hand, carefully pinch the clump at the edge of the cap and remove it. Handle stacked hair gently but firmly so as not to misalign the tips as you transfer it from hand to hand for the steps that follow. Remember that hair is cheap and stacking is quick and easy. If you mess up the first bunch, just restack it or cut a new bunch and try again.

32. To measure: Transfer the clump to your right hand and hold it against the hook with the tips of the hair toward the rear. Adjust your grip on the butt end so an entire hook-length of hair extends from your fingers to the left.

33. Transfer the clump of hair to your left hand, gripping it at the spot you marked above, and tie it in behind the eye, where shown. About an equal amount of hair will be sticking out to the front and rear of the tie-in point. (Tip: Before tying in, spin the bobbin counterclockwise to create twisted thread.)

34. Pinching the rear portion of the hair (the tip ends) with your left hand, wind twice around the clump to hold it in place, pulling up firmly on the bobbin after each wind.

35. Make 6 or 8 more wraps, pulling up tightly on the bobbin to flare the fibers.

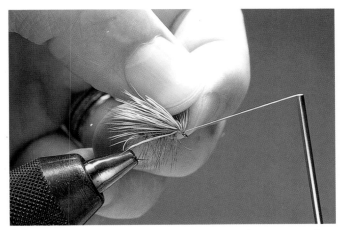

36. Now grasp the forward portion of the clump (the butt ends) with your left hand, pull it out of the way to the rear, and wrap twice forward of it.

37. Whip finish by forcing winds of thread tightly under the butt ends of the wing, and apply a drop of head cement.

38. Pinching the butts forward with your left hand, trim them above the eye, angling your scissors blades toward the rear, as shown.

39. Elk Hair Caddis.

Note that the wing and the clipped butts angle 45 degrees away from the hook in opposite directions and that there's a distinct gap between the two. The clipped butts may imitate the head of the caddisfly.

7

Compara-Dun and Sparkle Dun

Compara-Dun
Tail · Body · Wing

Trailing shuck

Sparkle Dun

The Compara-Dun style of hairwing dry fly was introduced by eastern tiers Al Caucci and Bob Nastasi in *Hatches* (1975), their ground-breaking study of mayfly patterns. The style imitates the dun, or sexually immature, stage of the mayfly. It is easy to tie and remains one of the most important mayfly dun imitations. Compara-Duns are tied in a number of colors to imitate various mayflies. The color used here approximates the species known to fishermen as sulfurs, pale evening duns, and pale morning duns. Pale morning duns (or PMDs) are the smallest of this group, typically occurring in size 14 to 18.

A simple variation is the Sparkle Dun, which imitates an emerger, the stage between nymph and dun, where the insect is shedding its husk, or "shuck," as it rises to the surface. In the Sparkle Dun, the forked tail of the Compara-Dun is replaced by a bit of Z-Lon to imitate the trailing shuck of the emerger.

Hook Standard dry fly, size 12–22.

Daiichi 1180, Mustad 94840, Tiemco 5210.

Thread Olive 6/0.

Wing Coastal deer hair.

Sometimes sold as Compara-Dun hair, this hair is fine and has short black tips.

Tail (Compara-Dun) Microfibbets, dark dun.

Microfibbets are a sturdy, finely tapered tailing material sold in a variety of colors to match specific insects.

Trailing Shuck (Sparkle Dun) Z-Lon, rusty brown.

Body Pale morning dun (PMD) or pale yellow natural dubbing blend.

You can buy preblended natural dubbing of rabbit, beaver, or muskrat, or you can mix a blend yourself from natural fur. As in the tail, the color you choose for the dubbing depends on the insect you're imitating.

Note: Before tying on, cut off a piece of thread 4 or 5 inches long and set it aside for use in Step 14.

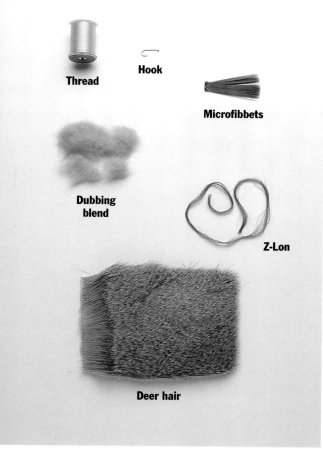

Thread · Hook · Microfibbets · Dubbing blend · Z-Lon · Deer hair

Compara-Dun / Sparkle Dun

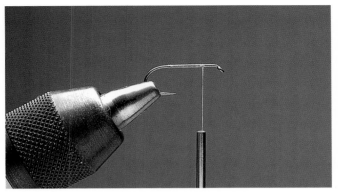

1. Tie on at the bend and wrap forward to about ¹/₃ shank-length behind the eye.

2. Cut and stack a bunch of deer hair, as in Steps 26–30 on pages 57–58. Holding the bunch in your left hand, tips toward the eye, adjust your grip so 1 shank-length of hair extends from your thumb to the eye. You've just measured the length of the wing and are gripping it at its tie-in point.

3. Move the bunch forward so the tie-in point is about one-third the length of the shank behind the eye. Tie in the bunch here with a pinch wrap and secure it with a few additional wraps of thread. Tip: Using counterclockwise twisted thread will make this process easier.

4. The deer hair tied in.

5. Make 8 tight wraps rearward to compress the deer hair. This compression will allow for a smoother body when thread is wrapped over the clipped butts.

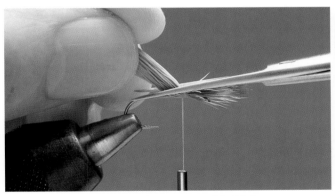

6. Wait a few seconds, then unwind half the wraps you made in the previous step and let the bobbin hang. Holding the butts of the hair up to the rear at the angle shown, and pressing down on the tips of the hair with the flat of the scissors blades, snip off the butts.

7. The trimmed butts.

8. Wind flat thread back over the trimmed butts to form a smooth taper.

To tie a Sparkle Dun, proceed with the next step. For the Compara-Dun, skip to Step 13.

9. Cut a 1-inch strip of Z-Lon, thin the strip to about one-quarter its diameter by removing strands with your fingers, and trim the ends square.

10. Tie in the Z-Lon with a flat-thread loop on top of the hook where shown, and then wrap rearward to where the bobbin is hanging in the next step.

11. Trim at an angle. About 1 hook-gap of material should extend from the end of the hook.

12. The completed trailing shuck of the Sparkle Dun.

To continue with the Sparkle Dun, skip to Step 18.

13. Tie in 3 Microfibbet fibers at the bend with a flat-thread loop, leaving a length about $1^1/2$ times the hook gap extending to the rear as the tail. Wrap forward to where the thread is hanging in the photo.

 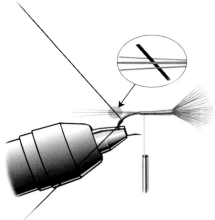

14. Take a piece of scrap thread about 4 inches long, loop it around the hook beneath the tail, and bring the far piece up between the middle and far strands of tail, as in the drawing.

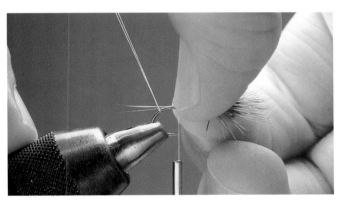 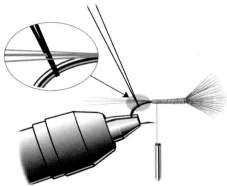

15. Bring the near piece of scrap thread up between the near and middle strands of the tail. The thread should now be on either side of the center tail strand.

 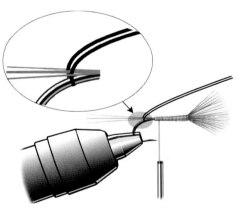

16. Pull the ends of the scrap thread forward to separate the strands of the tail. Pick up the bobbin and wrap 3 times over the base of the tails.

 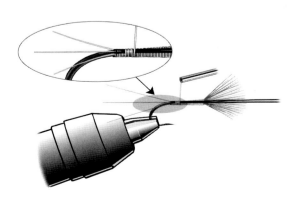

17. Trim off the tag ends of the scrap thread, and the tail is finished.

18. Twist a bit of dubbing blend clockwise onto the thread so that it tapers slightly from top to bottom. Leave some bare thread at the top.

19. Wind rearward to the bend, taking up the bare thread. Then wind the dubbed thread forward to 1 wrap shy of the wing.

20. Pull a fifth of the deer hair rearward, wrap once loosely around the gap, and then pull up firmly on the thread. This step and the three that follow will secure the wing in an upright position.

21. The wing after the first wrap is tightened.

22. Repeat the process in Step 20 three times, pulling a fifth of the hair rearward, wrapping loosely around the gap, and pulling up tightly. Finally, drop the thread over the shank right in front of the wing.

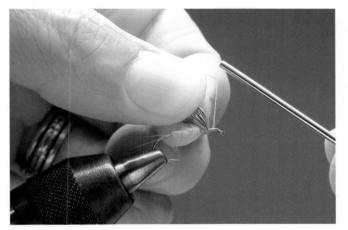

23. Holding the entire wing to the rear, wrap flat thread several times in front of it, building up a base to keep the wing from leaning forward.

24. The buildup of thread, along with the previous wraps through the middle of the deer hair, will keep the wing upright in the water when you fish this fly.

25. Pull a few more inches of thread from the bobbin and twist on dubbing.

26. Wrap the dubbing twice in front of the wing.

27. Bring the dubbing to your near side and over the hook, behind the wing.

28. Make a final wrap in front of the wing. If there are gaps in the body, repeat Steps 27 and 28.

29. Pick off excess dubbing, whip finish, and apply head cement.

30. Compara-Dun.

This is a simple, durable fly. Because its body has no hackle, a Compara-Dun rides lower in the water than most dry flies and is also less fragile. You can catch dozens of trout on one with no damage to the fly. Note how the wing sticks straight up.

Sparkle Dun.

Identical to the Compara-Dun, except for the trailing shuck.

8

Adams

Tail • Body • Wings • Hackle

Like the Gold-Ribbed Hare's Ear and the Woolly Bugger, the Adams is the most popular pattern in its category—in this case, the dry fly—because it imitates a variety of trout food forms and keeps catching fish. It was created by Len Halladay of Mayfield, Michigan, in 1922. In style it is a traditional Catskill dry, with slender body and upright, divided wings. It's been speculated that trout mistake the grizzly wings for the whirring wings of caddis adults taking off from the water, but the Adams also works well during mayfly hatches.

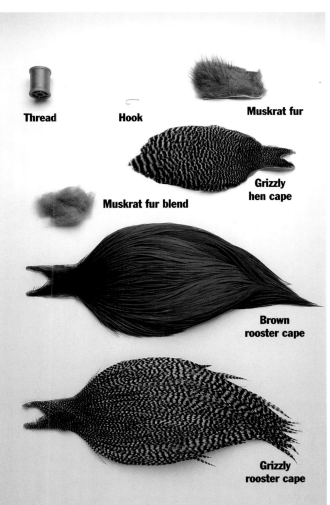

Thread • Hook • Muskrat fur • Muskrat fur blend • Grizzly hen cape • Brown rooster cape • Grizzly rooster cape

Hook   Standard dry fly, size 12–20.

Daiichi 1180, Mustad 94840, Tiemco 5210.

Thread   Black 8/0.

Wings   Hen grizzly hackle tips.

Feathers from a hen grizzly neck are shorter and broader at the tips than those from a rooster and thus are a better shape for these wings.

Tail   Mixed grizzly and brown hackle barbs.

You can use two rooster capes—a grizzly and a brown—as the source for the tail and hackle of this pattern. Or you can buy a split cape: half grizzly and half brown. The spade hackles at the outer edges of the cape are best for tails, because they are stiff and help keep the fly afloat.

Body   Muskrat fur blend.

Hackle   Grizzly and brown.

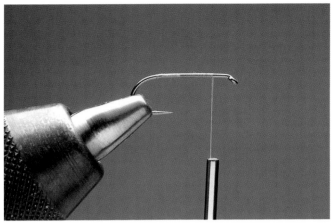

1. Tie on at the bend and wind flat thread forward to a few eye-lengths behind the eye. Let the bobbin hang.

2. Select a matched pair of hackle tips from a grizzly hen neck. The feathers should be no wider than the hook gap.

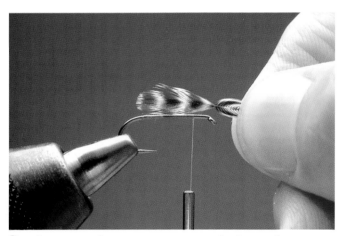

3. The wings should be as long as the hook shank. Measure each feather against the hook with the tip toward the bend, and mark their length by separating the barbs at the base. Strip the barbs from that point to the end, creating a length of bare stem for a tie-in point. (See next photo.)

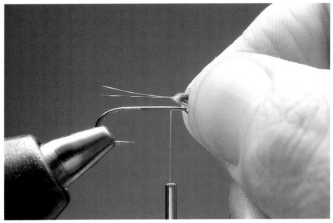

4. Turn the feathers around, even up the tips, and tie them in where the thread is hanging with a flat thread loop.

5. Make 4 or 5 wraps of thread rearward over the stems to hold them down. Trim the excess stems (extending to the left, above.)

6. Gather 6 or 8 barbs from a grizzly spade hackle and pull them up 90 degrees from the stem, as shown above. They should be about $1^{1}/_{2}$ times the length of the hook. Hold them by the tips and peel them off the stem. Set this clump aside—clipping the base ends in hackle pliers will keep the barbs from blowing away—and repeat the process with a brown spade hackle feather.

Adams

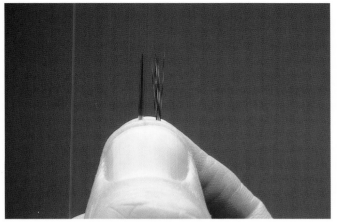

7. You now have a clump of grizzly and brown barbs from which to make the tail. Gently roll them together in your fingers to mix the two colors, and then even up the tips before going on to the next step.

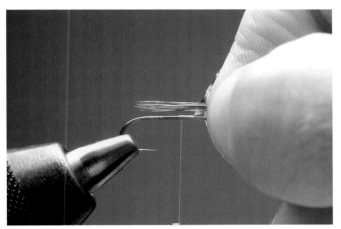

8. Hold the mixed tail over the hook and measure off 1 shank-length by pinching at the butt end at the appropriate spot with thumb and forefinger of your right hand. Notice how the brown and grizzly barbs are intermixed.

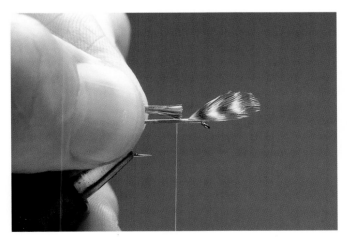

9. Switch the tail to your left hand, leaving the tips pointing left and gripping it at the place marked by your right hand in the previous step. Cut off the butts to the length shown, and tie in the tail at midshank using a pinch wrap.

10. Wind back to the bend with flat thread. Trim off the butts of the tail.

11. Cut a piece of muskrat fur from the hide from which to prepare dubbing. The guard hairs are the long reddish-brown hairs sticking out the top.

12. Hold the clump by the base and pull out the guard hairs by their tips.

13. The fur without guard hairs. Mix this fur according to the instructions for "blending by hand" on page 24.

14. Pull out about 4 inches of thread, let the bobbin hang, and twist on a sparse bit of dubbing using the single-thread method described on page 26, and slide it up to the hook shank. Your dubbing strand should be thin, like the one shown here, because the body of this type of dry fly is much more slender than that of a buggy nymph like the Gold-Ribbed Hare's Ear. Remember that a common beginner mistake is loading too much dubbing on the thread.

15. Wind the dubbing forward, stopping at least an eye-length short of the wing to leave room for winding the hackle. Pick any excess dubbing off the thread hanging from the hook.

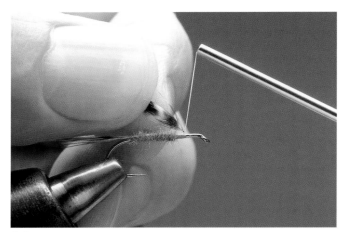

16. Wind the thread forward and, holding wings to the rear, wrap in front of them a few times with flat thread . . .

17. . . . so the wings are propped upright.

18. Select two hackle feathers, one grizzly and one brown. Match the barb length of these feathers as closely as you can.

19. To size the hackle, bend it in an arc so that the individual barbs on one side of the stem stick out, and hold them next to the hook gap. The barbs should be about $1^1/2$ times the gap width.

20. Strip some barbs from the base of the two hackles. Holding the hackles on the near side of the hook, shiny side up, tie them in just behind the wing.

21. Wind thread back just shy of the dubbing.

22. Wind thread forward, just behind the eye.

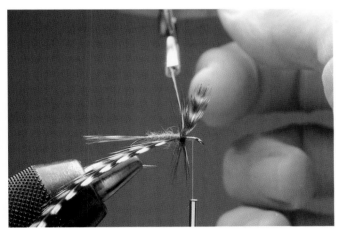

23. Grasp the tip of one hackle (here, the brown) with hackle pliers and wrap it behind the wing 2 or 3 times. Count the wraps, so you can do the same number for the other hackle.

Adams

24. Holding the wing to the rear, wrap the brown hackle tight against it and then forward 2 or 3 wraps.

25. Tie off the brown hackle with 2 wraps, but don't trim it yet. Let the bobbin hang there.

26. Transfer the hackle pliers to the other hackle and repeat the previous three steps. Note: Wrap this hackle the same number of times in front and behind the wing as you did the first one, so you get an even blend of grizzly and brown. Trim both hackles, and whip finish.

27. Adams.

This fly displays the proportions and profile of a traditional dry fly. The tail is about 1 shank-length long. The dubbing is slender, the hackle is wound as a collar at the forward part of the fly, and the mated pair of wings stick straight upright. Note the subtle blend of grizzly and brown in the tail and hackle.

9

Marabou Muddler

The Marabou Muddler is a variation of the Muddler Minnow, the classic sculpin imitation created by Don Gapen of Minnesota in the 1930s for brook trout in Ontario's Nipigon River.

This variation uses a marabou wing instead of the married turkey feather wings of the original pattern, and is somewhat easier to tie. The wing can be tied in a variety of colors, the most popular being black, olive, and yellow.

It should be drifted and retrieved through riffles and pools, with occasional twitches to mimic an injured baitfish. It is especially useful in pools or deep holes for large, carnivorous trout.

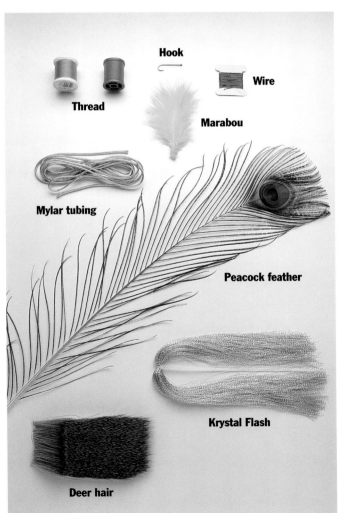

Hook	Streamer, 4X long, size 2–12.
	Daiichi 1750, Mustad 9674, Tiemco 9395.
Thread	Florescent orange 3/0, tan 3/0.
Weight	Medium-gauge wire.
Body	Mylar tubing, medium.
Wing	Yellow marabou, Krystal Flash, peacock herl.
Head	Deer hair.

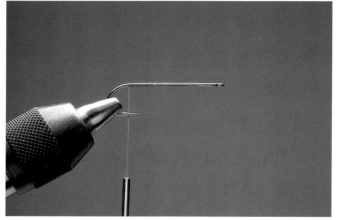

1. Tie on with orange thread about ¹/₄ shank-length behind the eye and wind back to just beyond the bend.

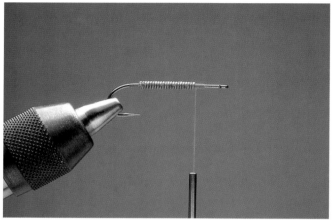

2. Wrap weighting wire around the hook (see Woolly Bugger Steps 4–7 on pages 30–31) and then wrap thread forward over it in diagonal wraps. With flat thread, build up level thread wraps at the front to keep the wire from sliding forward.

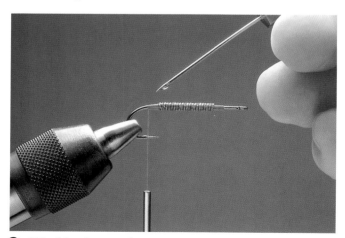

3. Wind back over the wire and build a taper on the rear side. Apply a thin bead of head cement over the body. This will take a minute or two to dry.

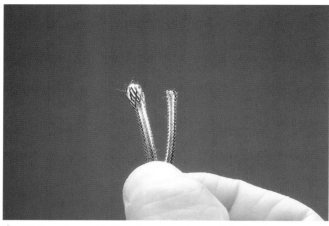

4. Using the middle of your scissors blades, cut a piece of Mylar tubing about as long as the hook. Trim the ends cleanly (right), not raggedly (left). Pull out the core material.

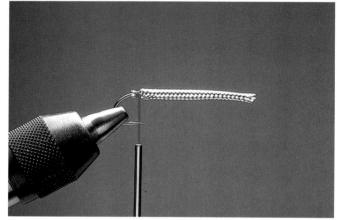

5. When the cement you applied in Step 3 is dry, slip the tubing over the hook and tie the back end on at the bend with 3 or 4 wraps of thread.

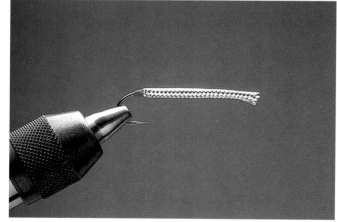

6. Wrap back over the end of the tubing, build up a tapered thread base, whip finish, and cut off the thread.

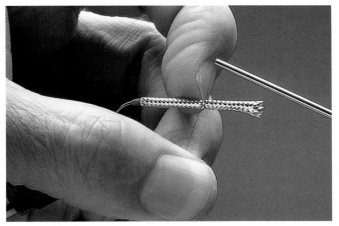

7. Stretch the tubing forward and locate the front edge of the wire with your fingernail. Tie in there.

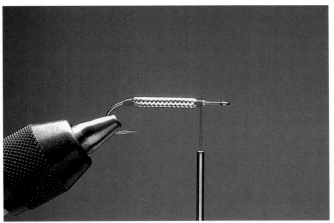

8. Trim off the excess tubing, just forward of the tie-in point, and the underbody is finished. Coat it with clear head cement.

9. Select 2 marabou feathers for the wing, preferably like the one on the left, with full, fluffy tips.

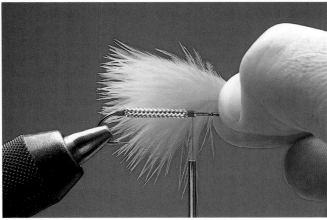

10. Match the 2 marabou feathers face-to-face and measure an entire hook-length with both feathers. Trim off the excess from their bases (to the right side of the feathers above).

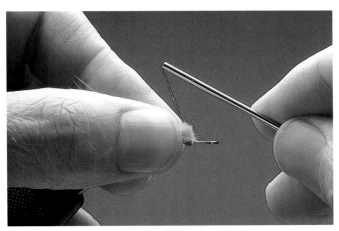

11. With the matched pair of wing feathers held horizontally, tie them in with 2 pinch wraps.

12. Make 5 or 6 more wraps over the wing butts to the front of the thread base.

75

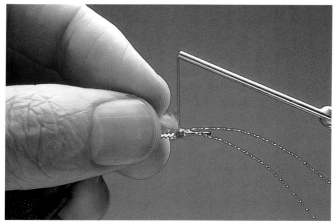

13. Select 2 few strands of Krystal Flash from the skein. Tie them in at the front of the wing (with 3 wraps of thread) so that their ends extend as in the next photo.

14. The Krystal Flash tied in.

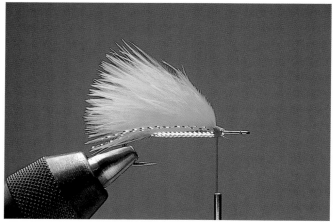

15. Fold the 2 forward strands of Krystal Flash to the rear on the far side of the hook and wrap twice at the front of the wing to secure them. Trim the ends of the Krystal Flash so one strand in each pair is a little longer than the other. This will give the strands more action when fished.

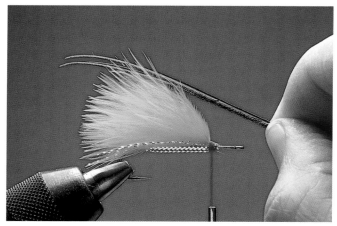

16. Cut 5 barbs ("herl") from a peacock feather.

17. Tie the herl in where shown, with the tips extending just past the tail.

18. Trim excess herl from the front, whip finish, apply head cement, and cut the thread.

19. When the cement is dry, tie on with tan thread a few eye-lengths behind the eye and wind back to the base of the body.

20. Cut, comb, and stack a bunch of deer hair, as you did in Steps 26–30 of the Elk Hair Caddis (pages 57–58). Measure off about 1 shank-length of hair against the hook.

21. Switch hands so that your left fingers grip the hair at the spot marked in the previous step. Cut off the butts where shown.

22. Holding the bundle over the hook, wind 2 loose wraps of twisted thread around it at a point just forward of the Mylar body.

23. Make a third wind, this time pulling tightly on the bobbin while letting go of the hair with your left hand. As the hair is released and the thread is wound, the hair will spiral around the hook shank.

24. Make 3 more winds through the hair butts, and let the bobbin hang.

25. Push back the tied-in hair with your right thumb and forefinger.

26. Cut and comb a second bundle of deer hair, just like the first, and trim off the tips. There is no need to stack this bundle. Holding the tied-in hair butts back with your left hand, as in the photo, lay the bundle on top of the shank and tie it in right in front of the hair butts, using the same technique as in steps 22–24.

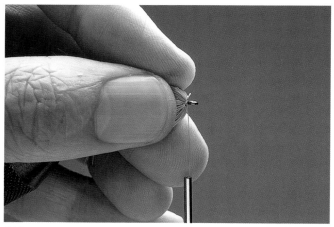

27. Pull the hair rearward, whip finish, and apply head cement.

28. Carefully break a double-edge razor blade in half lengthwise. Bending the blade to get the contour you want, shave the hair into a bullet-shaped head, as in the next photo. Scissors can be used instead, but a razor blade makes shaping quicker and neater.

29. Marabou Muddler.

Note the sleek profile of this streamer, which imitates a minnow. The Krystal Flash and peacock herl in the tail add light-catching highlights. The patch of orange thread peeking through may suggest gills or a wounded baitfish.

Resources

BOOKS

Basic Fly Tying, Ed Koch and Norm Shires. Stackpole Books.
Basic techniques, with chapters on tails, bodies, wings, and hackle.

Essential Trout Flies, Dave Hughes. Stackpole Books.
An expert's list of the 31 most important patterns to carry, with step-by-step tying instructions and fishing notes.

Guide to Fly Tying, Dick Talleur. Stackpole Books.
Dozens of patterns with detailed, step-by-step photos and explanations of technique. For intermediate tiers and beyond.

The Fly Fisher's Illustrated Dictionary, Darrell Martin. Lyons Press.
A comprehensive dictonary of terms, including historical entries.

Fly Fishing Basics, Dave Hughes. Stackpole Books.
A basic guide: gear, casting, pattern selection, stream tactics.

The Fly Tier's Benchside Reference, Ted Leeson and Jim Schollmeyer. Amato Books.
The definitive encyclopedia of techniques and dressing styles.

Fly Tying: Adventures in Fur, Feathers and Fun, John F. McKim. Mountain Press.
A technique and pattern book for beginners with superb black and white illustrations.

Hooks for the Fly, William E. Schmidt. Stackpole Books.
Listing of models from all major manufacturers, with cross-reference charts and descriptions.

Trout Flies, Dave Hughes. Stackpole Books.
The definitive guide to trout fly patterns, with tying instructions. 500 recipes in all.

MAGAZINES

The following national magazines, available at book stores and newsstands, have regular articles on fly tying.

American Angler
Fly Fisherman
Fly Rod & Reel
Fly Tyer
Flyfishing and Tying Journal

ORGANIZATIONS

Federation of Fly Fishers (*Flyfisher* magazine)
PO Box 1595
Bozeman MT 59771
406-585-7592
www.fedflyfishers.org

Trout Unlimited (*Trout* magazine)
1500 Wilson Blvd. #310
Arlington VA 22209-2404
704-522-0200
www.tu.org